Against the Odds
Memoirs of a Migrant
Worker

Order this book online at www.trafford.com
or email orders@trafford.com

Most Trafford titles are also available at major online book retailers.

Printed in the United States of America.

ISBN: 978-1-4269-0757-9 (sc)

*Our mission is to efficiently provide the world's finest, most comprehensive book publishing
service, enabling every author to experience success. To find out how to publish your
book, your way, and have it available worldwide, visit us online at www.trafford.com*

Trafford rev. 10/29/2010

 www.trafford.com

North America & international
toll-free: 1 888 232 4444 (USA & Canada)
phone: 250 383 6864 ✦ fax: 812 355 4082

Against the Odds

Memoirs of a Migrant Worker

Celia Castillo

PREFACE

I am an antique. Way back when I was in the classroom there was no phone, intercom or typewriter much less a computer for either teachers or students to practice innovative skills. When I wrote a mini thesis for a master's degree I read books at the university library took notes and that's how I researched. We did have access to newspaper articles which could be scrolled on a machine. I don't remember what the machine was called but much material needed to be scanned to find pertinent information. We did have one by twelve inch strips of film which could be viewed through a magnifying strip of glass but it was as helpful as the newspaper. I think we called that strip either ERIK or ERIC. What are the words to the acronym? I don't know. I don't remember which was more time consuming, the books or the machines but I came out with a professional product according to my strict thesis professor.

Often students in college came to me for help with their writing and I helped quite a few. I also helped some of my family with their higher learning assignments and that led them to believe that I could write. Wrong...or so I thought! Tell me what to write about, I will research and write. Give me a paper on which a professor has bled all over with a marker and I'll teach you how to correct it. Notice that I said teach. I will not redraft but I will help with redrafting and come out with an acceptable product. Help with technical writing, rhetoric and composition, those are my skills, but don't ask me to write from my head. Non-the-less my kids kept insisting that I write children literature, write Spanish children's books or write something, anything. Well, I couldn't convince my family that I can't write so I decided to write my own life experiences. I wrote and wrote and wrote, by hand, and this does not cover all the material I wrote. I didn't realize I had so much to share. Now what? Well I couldn't let all that material go to waste so why not share.

I had learned to type when I was about twelve because my father had rented a type writer for my sister who was graduating from high school and I was really into learning so I studied her chart and became proficient at typing. However, I didn't touch a type writer until umpteenth years later and that was just a few papers that I typed in college for my bachelor's degree. I typed those with my two index fingers so when it came to typing my thesis for my master's degree I basically relied on a typist. Following my thesis, I didn't do any typing. So there I was, with stiff fingers, computer illiterate and with a chronicle to be drafted. My girls helped, my grandkids helped, even my eight year old granddaughter got involved. My eleven year old grandson offered his illustrating talent but can you imagine an antique trying to describe an antique? No way! He tried to follow my description of antique items but to no avail. There went that idea. About half way through the whole thing, one of my girls showed up at my door, on Mother's Day, with a computer and said, "Type". I looked and stared at the monster. What do I do now? Please help! Luckily my daughter didn't leave me on my own and gave me a few starting pointers. To top it off another daughter gave me her printer and said, "Print". Now I had a computer and a printer. What else was I going to be bombarded with, People. And again, they didn't give up on me and they ended up helping more than I hate to admit. But let me tell you, there's no way I could have produced a book without my family's help. But please don't even ask about computer terminology. One good thing though, thanks to them I learned to pull up a blank screen, somewhat type, somewhat erase and somewhat polish my manuscript. I told you not to ask! However, I did realize how much of a novice I am when I was to start typing one day when my son came over and said: So that's what you call a blank page. I did all the writing though… by hand. Hurray for me!

Thank you, Thank you, Thank you.

I started to write, I just knew I knew how Leticia said yes, I'll help you tap keys.

With stiff untrained fingers, I made some mistakes. Brooke Caroline said "Grandma, deleting is easy - just mark it in blue, and hit the long key."

"Well how do you color and why not in red?"

Leticia said "Mom, just listen to her!"

Although she's just eight, her skills are supberb.

My grandson the artist, decided to help. He said "What's a book without illustration?"

I was totally thrilled what more could I want than eleven year old Alex, and his talented strokes?

But alas when I tried, to describe some antiques

I couldn't remember demensions exact.

He couldn't imagine, the weird strokes described. So much to our regret, there went that idea.

Until Leo chimed in, with an ingenious idea to import notable pictures for a memorable product.

At forty-one pages, Diana dropped in. She flew in to Texas, from Michigan State. She read all the pages and marked very few. She knodded approval before her adieus.

So now let's move forward, with a few final touches. For cutting and pasting, were yet to be done.

So thanks go to Sasha for offering help. All greatly appreciated so thank you again.

Two other grandchildren, and so did my son moved paragraphs forward and paragraphs back

(We finally finished, or so I believed)

But finishing touches, and editing skill were still in line waiting, so had to be done with Delphia's proof reading and corrected mistakes (which were very few) the product was ready to move on ahead.

Leticia's experience, in publishing steps came in really handy, and 'twas a relief. We all put in hard work, so you may enjoy a simple life story, in a plain little book.

In memory of my late parents, with love and gratitude.

Against the Odds
Memoirs of a Migrant Worker

By Celia Castillo

Part 1

The Farm

At the time, I was too young to understand but it seems that we left settled farm work and became migrant workers because of the lack of resources brought about by the "Great Depression." Growing up during that time, I experienced a significant change in our way of life together with my family of eight siblings and my parents. One constant was that we all worked hard, ate well and according to me, led a tranquil family life before, during and after the depression not counting external variables which had nothing to do with the economy.

About the depression going on in the United States there's not very much I can say except that the economy was low and jobs were difficult to secure. One significant memory that does stand out, in our case, is the rationing of certain items. As I mentioned, I was too young to understand any of it but I remember how we were allowed rations of some items based on the number of members in the family. Rations were in the form of vouchers but I don't know exactly how that worked. However, if I recall correctly, sugar and gas were two of the items on the list. Don't ask me why but I recall my parents sharing vouchers with the neighbors. Maybe it was because of the topic of conversation centering on them. I remember some of our neighbors coming over to ask whether we had leftovers of any kind of vouchers. Maybe we bartered – their leftovers for ours.

It seems to me as if overnight we left the farm moved into Lyford and started migrating. We started working in lower south Texas close to home and eventually followed harvest fields across the states in my father's best interest to keep us fed and clothed. We quickly learned to pack efficiently and carry essentials only so it wasn't too bad.

Consequently because of gas rationing, I remember that we always owned a vehicle which was well maintained and kept in good running condition. Once we even purchased a brand new, heavy duty truck. I'm not sure how my father was able to buy the new truck after we left the farm but I think we got it from a military auction. How my father learned about something like that and acted on it I'm not sure. We certainly didn't have access to the Internet in those days to search for auctions. I remember the very impressive shiny new forest green truck. Not bad for an uprooted family!

Once we even had a cute shiny black Model T which we cranked up to get it started but whatever vehicles we owned were mainly used for working purposes. For that reason, we had an abundance of gas vouchers even though fuel was rationed. But even though we owned a vehicle or even two, we kids, walked one mile to and from school whenever we were not migrating but so did the other community kids who went to school full time.

For the most part, however, there weren't too many automobiles in the neighborhood. One family two houses down and across the street from us always drove their two boys to and from school. Some mornings, while my younger sister Flor and I were walking to school, they picked us up and dropped us off at school. We must have shared fuel rations with them during the depression.

Hence, my early memories before we relocated consist of living on a farm which we owned as a family and we all worked alongside my father to maintain it. That life gave me comfort and offered peace and security. Farm life allowed me to enjoy leisurely solitary walks after school and on weekends. Sometimes I zigzagged briskly while hidden by tall corn stalk greenery without a care in the world. Other walks which were very pleasurable may not have been more than half a mile to and from but for me at that time and at that age seemed really far and wide. Nothing to get in the way of strolls in a cool breeze with clean fresh air after a rainfall for instance or the aroma of spring blossoms and other pleasant smells such as the scent of freshly plowed earth. Splashing in puddles after the rain was also a treat. Then the feel of little dust twisters as they came from seemingly nowhere and swirled around me. Also, funnels that were not so small and the thrill and excitement of running to meet them and with my right foot step right in the middle just to see them disappear. I was in control. I could dissolve them. But under no circumstances would I dissolve all of them. Some I just enjoyed. They were thoroughly enjoyable as I welcomed them with face uplifted toward the sky and with open arms, literally.

When working in the fields, I welcomed them that much more and thanked them for the uplifting clean air they offered. In the field they didn't pick up dust because of the crops, it was just clean fresh air. Aaah! No way would I dissolve such a welcoming delight. One cousin who worked in the fields with us, sometimes, did the same thing but shouted "Barbitas de oro!" Somehow that's very difficult to translate. Believe me. But to her and me twisters were so rejuvenating that they had to be God sent. They felt like a long, soft, heavenly beard swirling around us just when we really needed it.

One of the things I enjoyed aside from funnels after we started migrating was jumping on a truckload of cotton. Whenever the truck was either full or half full of cotton but too late for the gin trip it would be postponed until the following morning. But as long as there was enough cotton on the truck to jump on we had fun. Flor and I preferred a full truck load but half full would do. After dinner we would climb on the cotton and jump as on a trampoline for a while until we dropped. After that we would just lie on the cotton, relax and I counted stars. I just knew I could count them all if I just counted groups of ten at a time, mentally encircle those and go from there. I had already tried groups of twenty but that was too difficult. Ten would work better. After a few groups I would stop but of course I knew exactly where they were and where I would start the next time I was out there to continue counting. After I designated where I would start, I just enjoyed the cool evening breeze. Those have to be some of the most peaceful times of my life after we left the farm. Gaze at the stars and relax. At times like that I didn't miss the quiet peaceful evenings of farm life as much.

To make walking more interesting on the farm I came up with an ingenious idea. My father often purchased some type of molasses which came in half gallon cans. The reason he bought molasses was because sometimes my mother didn't prepare a "merienda" and he had to have his traditional afternoon snack. He poured molasses on a plate and had that with flour tortilla or bread. When the tins were empty I rinsed and saved them to make stilts. Close to the top of the can I cut two holes one across the other on each can. Then I ran twine through the holes, tied it, closed the can with its sturdy lid and those were my stilts. The looped cord came to somewhere above the knee. I had fun clanking around on my ingenious idea. At that time parents were not worried about the black market or violators so I walked farther and farther on farm easements or trails. When I got tired I draped my stilts over my shoulder and walked back home.

After that, my brother Jaime who was three years my senior made a true pair of stilts for himself. He took a couple of two by four pieces of lumber and nailed a triangular piece of board on each to step on and to carry him off the ground. Across the top he nailed a foot long piece of board to slip under his arms. I "borrowed" his stilts sometimes and had fun with them but it would drive him crazy and chased me around as if his life depended on catching me. I was agile and athletic so he couldn't catch me. He was usually easy going and calm so I don't know how I managed to rile him. To tell you the truth I didn't think I was doing something so unforgivable. It was just stilts and I didn't snatch them out from under him. Besides, I had given him the idea. Go figure.

In town there were no fields or isolated easements to call our own so leisurely walks were postponed until migrating sessions. There one of my pastimes became molding clay which I found in our back yard and got hooked on creating different things with it. I ended up creating a tea set for myself then food to go with it. Then my elder sister's husband Pablo gifted me a very pretty store bought tea set when he learned I liked tea parties. I played with my tea sets with one of my neighbors. I think at one time she became upset because I had won jacks, marbles and other toys from her. One other game we played was to try to break each other's spinning tops. What we did was to spin our tops at the same time and the one whose top lasted longer would try to break the other player's top by spinning over it. I didn't break her top but I did learn more yo-yo tricks and as for checkers and other games she wouldn't even go there. We were easily bored with boy games, anyway, so we played with my tea sets. She didn't like molding clay so we played with the items I had.

What I did when we migrated was that I hid all my dishes underneath the house along the two by fours which held up the floor and the house. The house was about sixteen or eighteen inches off the ground on stilts. I thought my treasures were very well hidden and safe there but one of the times when we came back from migrating all my wares were gone. I just knew my little neighbor had taken them but I didn't say anything. What may have happened was that she probably thought it was payback time and took my dishes in return for what I had won from her even though it had happened fair and square. Oh well. Life isn't fair and anyway I had all the squishy mud I wanted for another collection. I was a happy muddy kid again. After that she waved from her house to invite me to play jacks in the living room where her father sat embroidering pillow cases. I didn't see what else he embroidered because our friendship tapered off----dwindled. It became boring for both of us. That family didn't migrate and I think they made a living from embroidered items. I was only a kid but I knew his embroidery was beautiful and professional.

I started picking cotton on the farm and continued while migrating. That means I was in my pre school years. Usually fields were close to home or houses where we resided temporarily. At first I walked a few yards ahead of my father, picked cotton and placed it in piles for him to pick up as he went by. Soon after, I got a burlap bag with a sewn on strap, traveled with the family when the fields weren't nearby and shortly after went to the smallest canvas sack on the market. Burlap bags ripped easily but we had plenty of those. We got our potatoes in them but it must have been difficult to keep me in them anyway. I don't remember when I transferred to the commercial one but I do know I was very young. I also remember however that eventually if I picked five hundred pound of cotton it wasn't a very good day, eight hundred was good and only one time I remember picking one thousand pounds in one day.

By then we were picking cotton with its shell not without as before.

Part 2

Culinary

Before migrating and while on the farm I remember my mother's culinary talent which must have made quite an impression on me because I can remember it vividly. As I recall, she seemed to be forever cooking whether we were migrating or home. I don't know when she slept or whether she slept at all. It seemed like she never did.

Among other delicious foods, I distinctly remember her homemade empanadas with yams, pumpkin or carrots, depending on which edible crop we were working with at the time on the farm. She also cooked delicious squash porridge and sautéed fresh corn from the fields. We called that "esquite fresco" because plain esquite was popcorn which we got from the fields also. Some called it palomitas. The popcorn ears were smaller than regular corn ears. She canned tomatoes more so than other fruits or vegetables and saved dry corn for making corn tortillas. When she had exhausted all other varieties of cooking with fresh or semi fresh corn, she took the dry corn off of the cob by rubbing two ears together, washed the corn and boiled it in lye water. From there, she rinsed the corn at least twice and ground it several times on a "metate". The metate as I recall, was a slightly curved inclined plane which was created from speckled stone. It was about eight inches across and about sixteen inches long. It rested on three "knobs": two longer ones on the back and one shorter one in front. The grinding tool used on the metate was a four-sided "arm" called "la mano" and was tapered at both ends. It was also made from speckled stone and was about the size of a rolling pin. (Please don't quote me on the metate description because I haven't seen one of those things in decades, literally.)

The corn preparation usually took place outdoors where my mother sat on a short stool or bench. The lye water for cooking the corn was either boiled outdoors over a campfire or indoors on a wood burning stove if the weather was questionable. When she worked outdoors the white part of the ashes left around the camp fire after it died, she utilized as a cleansing agent for pots and pans even though she had a commercial cleanser. She preferred ashes for that purpose. She did…. really. I was there and I remember a little Dutch girl on the cleanser container before the next popular one came around. The traveling stove was a four-burner, very pretty green and white kerosene stove with an oven on the side. It was the height of a regular stove. I don't know when or where we got that green stove.

For grinding the corn my mother got on her knees on a solid walked-on patch of earth on the side of the house in the still of the morning and again in the afternoon. The outdoor corn preparation was done whenever she cooked the tortillas over a camp fire, weather permitting, otherwise she worked and cooked indoors. The kitchen floor was also earthen but it resembled shiny black granite because of water sprinkling and sweeping to prevent dirt from flying. After the corn was washed and boiled it was ready for grinding so my mother placed a handful of corn on the "metate" and sprinkled it with water. The corn would then be ground with the grinding pin and caught in a bowl at the low end of the metate. Due to the drying characteristics of maize, water was required throughout the tortilla making process. The consistency of the prepared "masa" (dough) for tortillas was similar to prepared biscuit dough. Once the entire content was ground she took a handful of dough at a time and patted it with both hands into perfectly round, flat tortillas. She dipped her hands in water several times for each tortilla patting. Nothing else was added to the corn so it became dry almost instantly.

The tortillas she made were the best tortillas anybody could ask for. As soon as tortillas started coming off the stove family tradition followed which meant having a long-awaited fresh hot corn tortilla directly off the griddle and butter was then added to it. That was a special appetizer especially for the grandchildren who came along later. My mother also made flour tortillas but not too often except for our lunch when we were in the field.

Nightly as a family, we enjoyed tortillas with dinner outdoors under the front porch of our home. We sat at a wooden table with benches while the breeze kept flies away. During inclement weather we watched the rain from the porch but ate indoors. Often, after a delectable meal, we went into the fields to gather sugar cane for dessert. Or we picked berries from a huge mulberry tree which produced the sweetest berries I have ever tasted. Well, I can't really say that because when we moved into town we had a mulberry tree with purple berries but our neighbor had one with white berries. They looked exactly the same except for the color. I'm tempted to say that the white berries were even sweeter than the purple ones.

At other times we gathered different types of wild berries for dessert. Two particular kinds of berries I remember are a small orange berry we called granjeno and a red one we called capulin. Those were about the size of a pea and grew on large bushes. Now that was a treat: To sit outdoors in the cool night breeze under the stars and enjoy sugar cane and other treats without a care in the world. Nights were peaceful and stars were extra bright. Wow! What a fun, simple and carefree life! My father may have had some concerns running through his head but it surely didn't seem like it. In short, life was fairly simple and tranquil, on the farm. If only I could turn back the hands of time to that tranquility, I would...definitely.

I went on a tangent but please read on. I'm back on track now, I hope, so back to the corn. Between the corn on the cob and the dry-tortillas-corn stage, the texture was good for making corn patties which we called "albondigas de maiz." My mother prepared them by grinding simmered kernels on the metate then she added water and made the masa into patties. The dough for the patties was not ground as finely as the dough for tortillas. Instead of frying, she cooked them on the tortilla "comal." My mother rarely fried food.

The comal was one of the round removable covers on the wood burning stove. That griddle went with us when we migrated because very importantly my mother needed it for tortillas and secondly for "quesadillas" and other foods. For quesadillas we kids took a homemade corn or flour tortilla, browned it on one side turned it and covered it with cheese. Then we took another tortilla which had been browned on one side, placed that over the cheese and browned both outer sides on the griddle until the tortillas were crisp and the cheese melted. Those were delicious. Besides quesadillas we also prepared snacks with flour tortillas which were similar to pizzas. We toasted a tortilla really well on both sides and topped it with food. That was also a very delicious, inexpensive and easy to prepare "pizza" snack.

My mother also made the very best biscuits and "pan de campo" both on the farm and after we started migrating. The pan de campo was about the size of a pie plate and similar to biscuits but not as thick or as fluffy. It was totally delicious but there is no way I could describe it and do it justice. The crust was smooth and toasty but the inside was soft and chewy. It didn't crumble so it lent itself to be filled with food for an easy to eat sandwich. Sandwich doesn't do it justice either. I liked it stuffed with pan fried potatoes instead of other food choices. (If you're thinking carbohydrates- no problem – we worked them off. No flab on any of us). The reason it was called pan de campo was because it could be cooked in a cast iron Dutch oven over a camp fire. Just writing about it gives me hunger pains and then I really crave for a good chunk of the scrumptious meal. I see it in my mind and can almost taste it.

Now I'll get to the point of the biscuit and pan de campo story. I didn't tell you it had a point. Did I? Well it does and here it goes. We lived just about a quarter mile from the railroad tracks after we left the farm. Since we, as a nation, were going through difficult times and we as a family were so close to the railroad tracks, we often got some of the vagabonds who hopped freight trains. They would jump off of the box car they occupied whenever the train slowed down for the town. They came to our door and asked for food. I'm thinking they asked for food because my mother prepared stuffed biscuits or pan de campo for my father to hand to them. They never turned them down. Was it poor man's food for them? For me it was delicious even though it was not a rarity so if they were hungry it had to be tasty for them also. Perhaps for them when they received a homemade generous morsel that stuck to their ribs, it had to be heavenly no matter how poor. They seemed to enjoy it and they did look famished.

For a while, I made pan de campo in the oven but got away from it and lost the knack for it. There's no recipe that I know of so there's no way I could conjure it up again. About two or three years ago I saw a newspaper advertisement about an all day pan de campo celebration. It would take place at a park in a nearby town but I haven't heard anything about it lately. It was fairly recent so pan de campo cooks are still out there somewhere. When reminiscing I can imagine little dancing sparkles and crackling sounds created by sporadic campfires under cast iron skillets at the park. That takes me back in thought to so many camp fires of my younger years.

According to me, my mother didn't cook or bake an unpalatable dish no matter how or where she cooked until she was older and her failing eye sight worked against her. She did well with daily simple foods but she often tried complicated dishes which did not turn out the way we were accustomed. She tried cooking whenever she knew we were visiting and supposed we would be starving from the long trip. That was after part of the family ended up in Arizona and three of us sisters had our own families and had settled in Texas. She was close to eighty years old when she tried to make tamales for us. We didn't have the heart to tell her they weren't very good but because of her attempt, we tried to enjoy them anyway. She tried and that's what matters.

My father rarely cooked but was very picky and meticulous about the food we consumed and everything else he did. He didn't bring home items like "menudo", "tripas", skin for "chicharrones" (pork rinds) or anything like that. Even ground beef was very rarely prepared at home, if at all. Although to be neighborly, he did buy kettle prepared pork rinds from our neighbor. He was the store owner across the street in Lyford.

Even in the cotton fields whenever he found a stray ripe watermelon he always sliced it to perfection, his way, as he did at home and called us in for the treat. He sliced the ends off first and then he cut three inch slices (about) lengthwise and stopped just as he got to the heart of the watermelon. He left about six unsliced inches at the bottom. Then he tapped on the top slice to loosen it, pulled it out and started sharing. After he got to the six inch bottom he started slicing the heart of the watermelon at about an inch and a quarter each and shared those portions. The heart slices were to "die" for. Because of that, to this day, I pick the biggest watermelon preferably from local vendors and often enjoy about two per week. In fact I don't know of any family member who would pass up a portion of sweet juicy watermelon at anytime, anywhere.

During watermelon season which for us in South Texans is quite lengthy, I don't even look at the so called personal sized watermelons.... personal for whom? Nowadays, if you're lucky you may still find sweet, juicy, delicious red ripe watermelons as those of yesteryear but it's rare as far as I know.[No offence] I really miss the old fashioned harvesting, picking and delivery method of vine-ripe fresh watermelons. Let's go back?

Given the fact that he was so meticulous, it stands to reason that my father took great care whenever he cooked which wasn't often. None-the-less, he did cook and introduced us to "barbacoa de cabeza". Barbacoa de cabeza according to my father fell in the same disallowed category as mentioned before so I didn't learn about it until I was about ten years of age when he first baked a beef head in the ground. We were not home. By then we were already migrating and were staying in a little frame unpainted house with bare wood that had never been painted inside or out. The house was amid brambles which had been chopped down low with a sickle and a small area around the house was walked-on, clear ground. Someone must have stayed there just before we occupied the premises. And as customary when we came to the empty houses we occupied while migrating, we cleaned and scrubbed really well before we moved in. There my father baked barbacoa twice, maybe trice, but not likely, and this is what I remember happening: He started a good hefty fire outdoors, gathered some rocks or stones, I don't know which and dug a hole in the ground but I don't remember how deep. Somehow, he wrapped the beef head really well after washing it. Other than an outer layer of burlap material around it, I don't recall the wrap material before that.

I sound like the kindergarten kid who said cooking "pesgetty" was easy. With teacher help they ended up with the recipe but I wouldn't try it if I were you: You put a pan with water on the stove, add spaghetti and eat it.

My father placed a generous amount of embers from the fire in the hole, placed the stones over the embers and nestled the wrapped head in the rocks. I think he added more stones, damp tea towels over or around it and covered it with the soil from the cavity. He left that overnight. In the morning the meat easily flaked off of the bone. Please don't try this at home unless you want to. Go ahead.

Unlike commercially cooked and sold barbacoa in which care is not top priority, my mother served only the leanest meat off of the head but no matter how lean, barbacoa is barbacoa and is still fatty. And because of that and because of selective food habits that I picked up from my father and my mother of course, I introduced it to my own family but that was about it – introduced it. I have to admit, though, we still enjoy barbacoa de cabeza once in a while. I don't bake it though. Should I try?

When my father baked it we really enjoyed it in corn tortilla wraps with avocado and tomato. For those who wanted it there was chile (hot sauce) to add to the taco. Chile was a combination of fresh or canned tomato, onion, salt and what we called "chile del monte" which was hot, spicy pepper berries from wild bushes that we grew at home. Actually, we didn't grow them. They just sprung up readily around trees or fences mainly. Those could be picked and dried in the sun to use whenever needed. My mother sometimes did that. Sundried they kept well for a long period of time and if I remember correctly, there was no difference in the taste of the ground berries for the hot sauce. Often my mother mailed sundried berries to my eldest sister Lupe after she and her family settled in Michigan.

Before I go on let me give you a bit of information about how Lupe got her name: My parents lost their first-born so they prayed that the next baby survive. If so the baby would be given a Virgin's name sake, therefore Guadalupe. Done.

I don't know why Lupe couldn't find the berries there. They owned a dairy farm and there were birds galore. Did birds not like those particular berries in Michigan? Because hypothetically, plants have to sprout from bird droppings otherwise why did bushes grow mainly in areas where birds perched around our house? I don't remember droppings around the bushes, though. Hmm?

The whole drying process wasn't easy. In fact, it was tedious. Picking the berries which were about the size of a bb as in a bb gun was tedious enough but then the berries had to be spread in a single layer to dry. Berries could be picked either green or ripe for immediate consumption but took less sun-drying time when picked ripe red. For drying, my mother placed a clean, soft cotton sack remnant in the sun and over that a layer of burlap material and then the berries. I don't know how often, but she shifted the berries around once in a while until she decided they were dry enough.

As I write, one thing that amazes me is the fact that I don't remember swarming flies, or flies at all, whether we were home or migrating. Did flies not rest on the berries or anything else food-wise that my mother prepared indoors or outdoors? Or were we not as paranoid as we are today where flies are concerned? Because I remember my mother making some type of cheese when we were on the farm and I don't even remember flies on that. I couldn't even begin to tell you how she prepared cheese but in my mind's eye I see a gourd-like wet cheese cloth hanging from a beam on our porch and I'm sure there were no flies around it. Even if there were several layers of some type of cloth there, there had to be some fly-appealing attraction to the "gourd". That thing sat there practically unattended. Where were the flies? Not that I would write gleefully about flies on our food but it's a mystery to me.

In Lyford, our little hometown which was just a few miles from the farm we left, we had an icebox for preserving food. We had to preserve food ....right? The icebox was wood fabricated and had an insulated compartment at the top for ice. Once in a while Flor and I walked a mile to town after school or on Saturdays to fetch a block of ice. The ice was about a foot-size prism-like block and was tied with a rope around it for transporting. We had an ice pick at home to chip ice off of the block for drinking water and such. That was the same icebox we had on the farm. I don't know why we walked to town for ice when we always had an automobile. Maybe we walked for ice because the men worked at whatever type of harvest they could find in the area while we were at school or on Saturdays. Yes, that must be it because one of the things I remember doing after school was slicing tomatoes and arranging those slices very neatly on a plate. Then I sprinkled them with sugar to enjoy and I know I didn't pick those tomatoes so the men must have brought them home. After we moved from Lyford to an area which offered harvesting for a longer length of time an ice vendor drove by with a truck-full of ice and we purchased our ice from him. That was Robstown.

Can you believe that in 1949 we still owned and used an icebox and that I don't even remember when we purchased a refrigerator? Because of that for the longest time we referred to the fridge as an icebox and in turn, the electric bill was referred to as a light bill. That was because when we first installed electricity at home it was mainly a light bulb together with a plug outlet at the ceiling with a string to pull to turn the bulb on and off. Neat huh!

While migrating, it wasn't very difficult to keep food from spoiling because we were usually further north during fall and winter where the weather was cold or cooler. If the weather became warm or hot my father purchased two blocks of ice as needed. One block was for the water barrel we always carried with us and the other block was wrapped in some type of insulating material for our food, drinking water and such. Sometimes we made snow cones by scraping ice off of the block with an ice scraper, placed it in a cup and added snow-cone syrup. Ice was an essential part of our life back then. But during winter we could have definitely done without it on our drinking water when in the fields. Brrr!

Part 3

They Were Them and We Were Us

I recall that I started school and rode the bus when we lived on the farm but shortly after moved into town. My youngest sister Beatriz was born on the farm, as I recall. The first few years of schooling my siblings and I attended a little segregated "Mexican" school which was a mile away but a school bus was not afforded. At the end of our neighborhood which was called "Mejiquito" (Little Mexico) stood our Catholic Church. And just about half a mile down after an isolated area and toward town stood the Protestant Church. Across the street and a little way down there was a shortcut to school across a little park. Whenever the fruit was ripe I had my fill of dates from palm trees at that park. Those dates were really tasty. There were dates on other palm trees around the same area but those were not as sweet. A little farther down there were business establishments and a predominantly Anglo community to the right when facing south.

Wait....let me think a minute here. Come to think of it, I'm not sure the parishioners were a protestant denomination at the mentioned church but it was white people, so to me, they had to be protestant. As a kid I believed all Anglos were protestant.

What I would like to do some day if I'm ever in that area again is that I would like to stop and see what the "Protestant" Church looks like inside. But I don't know whether I would feel comfortable. It still stands, it still looks as sturdy as it did back then and it still seems functional even after about sixty years. It's a red brick building. The Catholic Church is a white frame building and it still stands also. I'm really curious to see what the inside of the red church looks like. While there I will also visit the Catholic Church.

There were no white business owners except the little convenient store where I worked the register but it wasn't in town and catered mostly to travelers. The main grocery store which offered limited ready wear, the department store where I also worked and a small store that catered mostly to students were Hispanic owned and so was the shoe repair shop. I never knew who owned the movie theater but the owners had to be Hispanic because they held some type of gong performances and those were in Spanish. Anybody who thought they had talent could get on stage and perform. One time one of the boys I knew got on stage and sang. I never knew he had talent until he got on stage. He was really impressive, talented and handsome also.

In our neighborhood there was a meat market with very few grocery items and a small store which offered non-perishables, basic staples and a lot of candy and sodas. There was a store across the street from our house and one at the end of that block. It's interesting that all stores in town were Hispanic owned. I wonder why? I'm sure they benefited from that but I still wonder. Where were the white people? We didn't see them.

Why was the meat market on our side of town? It was a clean, well-kept store and offered a variety of fresh quality meat. I know because my father was very particular about food and he purchased quite a bit of meat at that store. At times he asked me to pick up a few pieces of round steak because he knew we would get quality meat even if he didn't pick it up himself. He didn't ask me to buy any other type of meat. How rude.

I liked looking at the rows of fresh meat as the butcher picked up and wrapped the amount we needed. I was about nine the first time I went for meat. The store was just a half block away but I felt so proud because I knew what kind and how much meat we needed. That was after my father told me what to order but let's keep that a secret.

I don't think white people patronized the meat market unless they had their meat catered but I don't think so. It was evident that the owners did well anyway but they were down to earth neighborly people. One of the girls was a bridesmaid at Miguel's and my sister-in-law's wedding. Miguel was the elder male in the family.

Our school was across and away from the business part of town and everything else. The main highway and the railroad tracks separated us from both the town and the grammar school including the high school building and the White community. The school was basically isolated while the others were situated in close proximity to the business area and very convenient to the predominantly Anglo area of town.

The school was brick and the rooms were basically four frame walls. The other schools were totally brick. We did have indoor plumbing even though it was situated at the far end of the building and we entered the facility from the outside, rain, shine or sleet. Other schools had indoor plumbing. I'm sure the white community had indoor plumbing also but our neighborhood didn't. There were no sewer lines there. We had an outhouse which had to be white-washed with lye water, soap and scrubbed with a broom at least once a week. The wooden slatted path leading to the outhouse which was as far back as the property allowed didn't get washed as often but was washed at least twice a month.

To get to our elementary school we had to be extra careful when crossing the highway and railway because there was heavy traffic of both commercial and private vehicles and there was no school-warning sign to slow down the speeding traffic. There were no crossing guards either. We just had to take our chances when crossing the highway with speeding semis and when crossing the railway with speeding freight and passenger trains. Trains tooted and slowed down but not significantly. I was only six or seven years of age and there I was running across a highway and railway trying to beat traffic so I could attend elementary school! To walk to and from school was one mile each way. I remembered to take an odometer reading the first time I visited Lyford. I did that because often as we grow older we tend to "stretch" the miles or make the tale a little taller. It was one mile. I measured it. Where was our automobile? The men started out early to scrounge for work.

As I recall, students at that school carried flour tortilla "tacos" for lunch and they were really embarrassed to pull them out of the lunch bag to eat. They held the bag close to the mouth and took a bite of the taco without allowing anyone to see what they were eating. Having a rolled up tortilla with food was embarrassing. I wonder why? There were no white students at our little school. The teachers were white though and they ate at their desk. I don't remember a teacher's lounge and I don't know whether they could have their lunch at the principal's office. I carried biscuits stuffed with food. I didn't think that was embarrassing. The high school had a cafeteria and it was walking distance from the grammar school so students didn't carry a lunch there.

In retrospect and on top of all that I don't see the logic in attending a segregated school. We were Spanish unilingual but were not allowed to speak Spanish yet there were no Spanish or bilingual speaking educators to ease the transition from the Spanish to the English language. All teachers were Anglo unilingual speakers of English in public but some may have spoken a different secret language at home. Also, some of us were migrant workers which meant we missed partial academic sessions but there was no catch-up program for anyone. Go figure.

Here's something to ponder at leisure or possibly fume about. You know how sometimes we say that something that happened that's not very funny will be funny years from now or happened years ago and we can laugh about it now? Well here's something that happened decades ago and I had blocked it out of my mind. It surfaced as I write and I may have nervously chuckled because to me it's not funny and it may never be funny and here's why: The teachers at school taught us that we couldn't get up from our seats or talk without raising a hand to ask permission for whatever we needed. We obeyed and sat quietly during class time but one day one of the boys really needed to leave the room I suppose because he raised his hand and asked to go to the restroom….in Spanish. The teacher must have guessed what he needed and told him to say "May I be excused" whenever he needed to leave the room. What we heard, logically was "May I go to the biscuse" so that's how we asked to be excused from then on and for a long time after that. Luckily we didn't embarrass ourselves very often….we sat quietly during class time. How funny is that? Now I have a question…. several in fact. How could the teachers allow us to do that? What were they thinking? Were they thinking?

Did they think it was funny? There should be no excuse for that. Were they certified educators? I'll be a sport and give them the benefit of the doubt. Maybe they didn't exactly hear what we were saying because we were very soft spoken…. timid maybe? So maybe I'll manage to laugh some day. I can't foresee it but maybe…..someday. Are you laughing?

Another memory that pops into my mind when reminiscing is how I thought the school was huge. As an adult, I've stopped to see my school twice whenever I've gone by Lyford and was surprised to see how tiny the school really was. At one of those times I picked up a brick as a souvenir. I still have that brick. The little school is dilapidated now but no longer isolated. The community has spread around it. Not that I would want it bulldozed but I wonder why the debris is still there.

Even though I attended school only part time there each academic year I have an abundance of memories but I'll only mention a few others: I listened, learned and obeyed because I learned that if I messed up the principal would walk outside to the water fountain. (Yes, it was outdoors and the water was really hot sometimes.) He would wet his hand and spank the students who didn't tow the line. That was the norm for the girls and I didn't want that happening to me. Come to think of it, I don't remember the norm for boy's misbehavior punishment. Huh? Anyway I really liked school and was truly interested in learning. Beside, getting spanked at school could mean getting spanked at home for the same goof up. I didn't think it would be very much fun to receive a double dose.

Standing there in front of the dilapidated building on my first stop-over I see that part of the steps and the little platform we stepped onto before walking into the classrooms are still there. I still remember playing jacks on that platform as if though it was just yesterday and I remember being very competitive at it. Often we played for keeps and I ended up with gobs of jacks. Yet, I remember how one day I felt so rich because my father had given me six cents – a whole nickel and a penny – to spend as I pleased and I was going to buy more jacks with part of that money. Well, I went to the restroom which was waaay at the other end of the building and left my money there. Remember, we had to leave the rooms and walk on the outside of the building so when I realized I didn't have my money I turned around and ran as fast as I could back to the restroom. The money was gone. Part of that money was for jacks, as I said, even though I had so many. But the more you had the more popular you were, the more others wanted to play with you and the more you could pile up if you were talented at playing and won. Like I said, I had gobs of jacks.

During that visit to my little school I also remembered a pair of green socks that I wore out at the ankles and my sister Lupe patched them up with a different torn pair of red socks. I was so proud of those socks with the two pretty colors. Red and green! I would let my loafers slide off of my feet when I walked just to show off my pretty socks. In my mind's eye I can virtually see the happy little girl showing off the pretty socks. Red and green!

In contrast, I also thought about a big bully girl who was twice my size and was always picking on me. (I had long ago forgotten about that one.) One day I got fed up, forgot I was small and skinny and went at her. I rammed head first at her belly. I gave her some good punches and slaps while we both rolled around on the ground before the teacher came out to the playground and pulled me off of her. If I had known she would leave me alone after something like that I would have done it much sooner, double dose or not. Needless to say, the teacher kept us in after school for what seemed an eternity. Once she let us out I darted out of there, ran like crazy and panting breathlessly caught up with the other kids just before they got home. I was so grateful for that mile between school and home that day. My father never learned about that incident. Whew! He would have been so embarrassed and disappointed in me for fighting at school. And for being punished?! Oh my gosh!

I don't remember my father spanking me but just the thought of having to sit in front of him until I explained or fessed up was enough punishment. Sometimes he would walk away from where we were sitting but didn't dismiss me then he'd come back and sit again. I never doubted he would spank me though. Again in retrospect, I think he just walked away to chuckle because he knew I was a good kid and only needed a reminder on respect and obedience once in a while. I wish I had known that back then. What would I have done if I had known my father wouldn't spank me? I wonder. As for my mother, don't even ask about her. She lived with a belt draped around her shoulder. It was part of her attire.

Now I chuckle when I remember my father's unusual sense of humor which is amusing now but at that time we didn't quite understand it. Once for instance my youngest sister Beatriz said something he didn't approve of so he went straight to an electric pole to uproot it and spank her with it. She took off as fast as her skinny little legs could carry her. When she looked back to see whether he was at her heels he was just standing there all calm and collected. All she had said was: "Tengo una sed de perro amarrado." I didn't see anything wrong with that. The child was thirsty. Just give her a dipper of water. After that we got away with saying: "Tengo una sed {o hambre} como la sed de Bea. With me he once picked up a mop to spank me with and I took off like the wind so he couldn't catch me. Yeah right. The truth is that he never intended to catch me or any one of us. We reminisce now and laugh about similar ridiculous occurrences and his silly sense of humor. We have fun reminiscing and it's funny now.

After the third grade at the segregated school we went to grammar school and I have good memories from there. Teachers were really strict, I learned quite a bit with them and became very good in sports both in volleyball and what was back then called baseball although it was for girls.

From the fourth grade through the sixth grade I vied for first place with the top student in the class both academically and in sports. That is one student in particular whose given name I still remember to this day. Besides holding the top-student spot academically she was the pitcher for the competing grammar school team. I tried out for the pitching position, got it and ended up as the pitcher for the sixth grade year. Academically, for that year her report card and mine reflected equal achievement and quantity of marks. My Anglo competitor and I were basically the same size, both pretty trim, but I was stronger. With all the exercise I got in the fields she stood no chance of winning so I held a full time pitching spot for that year. That was one year we didn't migrate because my sister Gabriela who was the third born sibling was graduating from high school. That year my father decided that women and children would remain home while they went to the harvest fields.

My father didn't allow me to wear shorts and didn't condone participation in sports competition but I needed a uniform since I was on the traveling team now for both baseball and volleyball. We went on school tournaments so to give me a chance at participating, my mother sneaked out some white material to a neighbor seamstress for my uniform. The seamstress did a very professional job and tailored the shorts to fit perfectly. I hid those under a skirt until I actually played even though they came down to my fingertips when I stretched my arms alongside my body. The top of the uniform was white and had a bull pup imprint on the back. How did my mother do that?! The material for the uniform came from my elder brother's white Navy uniform. Our school colors were green and white and I really don't know how my mother completed my uniform or how she got the green ribbon that covered the seam and the zipper along the side of the shorts. I loved that uniform and felt very special and important in it.

At the time I really didn't understand the significance of what my mother was doing by supporting my competitive side. She afforded me the opportunity to play and even provided me with a uniform in which to play. That took courage. She was taking quite a chance allowing me to be me in sports in spite of the confrontation she may have had if I had gotten hurt and my father had discovered what we were doing.

Afterthought: I wonder what would have happened if Miguel had been in the Army instead of the Navy. Where would my mother have obtained the white material for my uniform? I guess luck was on my side. Huh?! The way I see it now is that she would have found a way to fulfill an academic need.... I'm sure. But you know what? The material wouldn't have been as nice as the Navy uniform material. My laundered school uniform looked extra expensive. Oooh, big time player! Get out of the way!

My father took care of the business aspects of home, family and work and my mother took care of domestic aspects of home, family and work. That's the reason I said that I don't know how my mother managed to clothe me in a uniform or how she kept my father from learning that I went out on tournaments. It helped that competition happened during school time, permission slips were not required and my father was gone for a few months for harvest. Now and in retrospect, I remember that my father thought participating in sports was dangerous and he didn't want me getting hurt so in a sense he was merely being protective of me. But I wanted to play so we cheated.

Twice during the sixth grade academic year I interacted with two different white classmates. One was the minister's daughter who was the catcher for the baseball team. She was not as popular as other girls, I thought, so I decided to go over and practice pitching the ball to her. I knocked on the door, she opened it, saw the ball in my hand, came out to practice but didn't talk. The only thing she said was that I was pitching the ball too hard so I tried to ease up. After about half an hour her mother called us in for cookies but didn't stay to chat. I then left, walked the mile back home and that was the end of that.

The other time I interacted with a white girl happened when we were picking cotton for one of the local farmers. The farmer had come over to talk to my father at the weigh station. The farmer's daughter who was one of my classmates came over with her father and happened to be there when I got to the scale. I said hello and told her the water was cold after I took a sip and that was the extent of the interaction.

To that I say, how was I supposed to practice my limited English? Even the teachers who were Anglo didn't talk to white students very much at school either. By then there weren't very many brown students in the sixth grade class and none from my neighborhood that I can remember. So because there was no one to practice English with at school and the few browns that attended were accused of being rude because whites didn't understand Spanish there was not much interaction among us. If we spoke Spanish it was rude because we were talking about whites. That was not true at all. There was no reason to. It didn't matter whether whites were schoolmates, classmates, or other, because they were an entirely different entity that did not concern us. They were them and we were us. That was something we had been taught and learned very early on. They really were invisible.

One good thing though, because the teachers at grammar school were strict I learned to like writing and that was a benefit as I continued with education. I didn't know the value of studying under dedicated educators then but it helped later through the years.

For their dedication in math which was called arithmetic, I have to give much credit to field work even though math teachers were also dedicated and strict but I will tell you about it later. Thanks teachers! *(One of which I became myself.)*

By-the-way, I had the worst trouble learning to spell the word arithmetic. That was a problem because perfect headings were required for all assignments back then. I did learn the trick to spelling it but first I had to learn a phrase then use the first letter of each word in the phrase. The phrase was: **A Rat In The House Might Eat The Ice Cream.** How about that?! Just between you and me, I still use it to make sure I spell the word correctly. But please don't tell anyone.

Now here's a draw-back in education because of learning differences. Reading was a whole different story in part-time classroom schooling. Basically back then we were educated in what was called the three R's which was Reading, wRiting and aRithmetic. I was learning computation skills while migrating therefore I mainly needed education in reading and writing areas. That's what I was talking about when I said I attributed mathematic skills to migrant learning and not necessarily or totally to teachers in the classroom.

Reading in the classroom after elementary school wasn't very effective for me. My unconventional learning style did not fit in with formal education at the time. At home I munched and reclined while reading. Also I read mainly for pleasure and read more Spanish than not. In the classroom it was a tombstone-like setting and upright sitting. There was no talking at all while reading silently but I could look out the window from behind my book. It was more interesting out there. But the problem was not with reading it was just that I wanted to relax comfortably while I read the way I was accustomed.

We didn't read orally in the classroom very often but it was better than reading silently. When we did, I knew when my turn would come up alphabetically. That didn't give me much time to regurgitate because my surname fell in the third letter of the alphabet. When we read by next- in- row procedure I often had more time to study my corresponding page so according to the teacher I read well.

I did acquire reading skills but not reading comprehension as well as I should have unless it was Spanish or pleasure reading. I do have an advanced level of intelligence so learned skills and concepts did help with transition as I learned more and more English. For a while I was up to par again.

I got along alright in grammar school but unfortunately I had dropped out of school so that means I cut formal education abruptly. At one point during migrating years schooling became mandatory or maybe it had been but we just didn't hear about it. The odds were against me. My three younger siblings fell within the mandatory age group. I didn't. I continued the fields; they went to school. When we moved to Robstown they also had the good fortune of attending a little migrant segregated school which I imagine gave them catch-up instruction. Again I didn't qualify. At the high school level there was no sink or swim option. It was just sink and nothing else. I couldn't advance on grades alone any more. I needed to accumulate a certain amount of academic credits. I was young. The teachers at Lyford elementary had decided I could jump from first grade to third so I was studying one grade level ahead.

Because my father insisted that I attend classes when we were home I tried two part time sessions for the required points to catch up but it seemed like it would take a lifetime to graduate. I would have one foot in the grave by then. I asked to drop out. But no way! My father was unyielding. It took a few days of begging and a good explanation before he relented and I dropped out. Formal education was cut short. Now what?

SCHOOL DAYS 1949-50

When I was able to continue with education, I attended only three classes of which would prepare me for a general equivalency diploma test. After the third class the instructor advised me to take the required test, I took it and scored really well with no problem. I was ready for the test, yes, but wasn't totally prepared for college English. I couldn't go back so I went forward. There, I started with a stack of assignments in one hand and a dictionary attached to the other. We didn't have the little hand-held computers for looking up word meaning or spelling, otherwise I would have concealed one in my pocket and nobody would have been the wiser. Fortunately I had no problem with mathematics so I was able to dedicate more study time to lacking areas and was able to make progress.

Ironically however, I had learned to spell in my younger years but lost the skill in college because of rote learning practice at school. Phonics concept came in later. Even though I had to hold my hands behind my back and write the assigned word on my left palm with my right hand index finger I succeeded when we had spelling bees at school. When it came to college requirements, however, I took a mandatory speech class which set me back. I thought I was there already. Oh well.

I won't go into detail but I will give you an example of what the class entailed: We received a vocabulary list as one of the assignments and were required to phonetically code a corresponding group of letters for each word's pronunciation. For instance, the word music if written the way it sounded would be something like MIYUZIK. I did learn to pronounce the word music correctly among other words but there went my spelling skills I had worked so diligently to attain. One step forward and two steps back. That's pretty consistent with the story of my life as it pertains to education. I'm really an okay speller now, not great but pretty good. I didn't utilize SUFIZTIKAIRIT vocabulary in my narrative but I didn't consult the dictionary too often.

Part 4

Ailments and Cures

Thank the lucky stars we were a very healthy family and were able to succeed on the farm, in our migrating and other vital efforts. In fact we may be able to attribute health not only to luck but also to the fact that we walked wherever we went except to work, the healthy environmental ecology and eating habits. For that reason, I suppose, the only "medication" I remember during the twenty-two years I lived with my parents were mentholated rub and whole nutmeg which my mother gave us to chew for an upset stomach. That didn't happen very often. She also brewed a tea from a plant she grew herself. That was for belly aches. Maybe I didn't get a queasy stomach because sometimes I sneaked into my mother's stash of "medication" and grabbed some nutmeg to chew on. I did, even when I had to climb on a chair to get it. When I saw my mother giving nutmeg to my siblings I wanted some also even though I wasn't ill. I just liked nutmeg. Is it good? I haven't tasted it in a very long time. Is it good? We had faith in our medication. But was it an inauthentic substitute for the "real" thing that was on the market? Should we have gotten medication over the counter? Was it worse than what we are taking now from commercial shelves? Hmm? All I know is that I wouldn't mind growing the tea herb if I could find it. I would just brew the tea and enjoy it—belly ache or not.

I should have researched before it was too late to learn about the herb that probably doesn't even exist now – but I didn't. I'll just tell you what I remember about it and try to put it in written form for you. Maybe you've heard about it before: It was a kind of grayish, whitish, dull-looking plant that my mother called "istafiate." The plant grew about two feet tall and wasn't bushy. It was just long slim-like leaves that grew basically straight from the stem itself and kind of pointed up. I may say this again, but please don't quote me because when it comes to items like that it's only what I remember – not facts.

When we were home, not following the harvests fields, my mother brewed the fresh plant; when we were out migrating, she carried a handful of the herb that she sundried for her tea. According to her it was more effective if it was taken straight – no sugar, no honey – and whether it was brewed from a fresh or dry plant didn't matter. Without sweeteners it was yucky. Yuck! I tasted it. I would add sugar to my tea if I could find the herb and brew it.

Another "cure" for ailments was for aches and pains as in the start of a cold, influenza and/or overworked muscles. That remedy was my father's forte for sure cure. He would have the ailing person clasp hands behind the neck with elbows level to the shoulders and draped his arms around the "patient". He then clasped the elbows with his intertwined hands and pumped the patient up and down a few times with feet off the floor. Often I could hear bones popping. I didn't allow him to do that for me because he was too strong and muscular. I was afraid my bones would do more than pop. Flor said it gave her relief from aches and pains and that I was missing out on a sure cure for aching muscles but it wasn't for me. No way! Bones popping.... I don't think so!

I was basically the healthiest kid in the bunch who never caught anything but I was the one who suffered more from ear infection and the only one who ended up with a serious illness – rheumatic fever. But I don't think it had anything to do with migrating phenomena. I was in my pre or early teens then. I just started with a swollen ankle and my father blamed it on physical education at school. Thank goodness he never learned about my participation in grammar school sports. I wonder if my mother worried about that even though my illness had nothing to do with it. I hope not.

One of the neighbors said it was more than a sprained ankle but then the swelling went down and it was forgotten until I got a swollen wrist; later a swollen knee. That was when my father thought it was best to take me to a doctor. He and I went by bus instead of our own automobile because he drove but he preferred not to. Now that I think about it maybe we did run out of fuel vouchers once in a while. Hmmm?

We went to the nearest doctor who was in the next town five miles north of us, Raymondville. I don't remember medication but I was to remain in bed and was restricted from exercise for at least six months. That was pure torture for a child who enjoyed school, loved to walk and play ball and other games with neighborhood kids.

After a couple of months of rest and no recurring swelling I gave myself permission to walk around the room from window to window. Well, the swelling came back and my father took me to the doctor one more time. He was told that if the swelling crossed the body I would not survive. The swelling had occurred something like this: The right knee or ankle and right wrist became swollen then the same on the left side. If the swelling was to cut across such as right knee, left wrist, for example, I wouldn't stand a chance. The doctor also told my father that stress had to be kept to a minimum or

I would not live to be twenty-five. The only thing the doctor said to me was to rest and try not to cry too much. He probably thought he had to keep it simple for me so that I would understand what I needed to do to beat the illness as per instructions. That was one of two times that I saw my father cry once we got home. He kneeled by the bed, took my hand, formed a ball with it and tried to dry his tears with it but there was no way he could do that. His tears rolled down all around my hand.

After I saw my father cry, I decided I'd better stay in bed. I did get well and didn't get swollen joints but my doctor said that if I got to the age of twenty-five the swelling would not return, probably, but the heart would suffer the consequences of on-going stressful emotions. Life is tough though and there is no such a thing as an unstressed life, I think. I've tried to live one day at a time but, nonetheless, I've learned that I have a scarred heart valve. My doctor now recommends that I take preventive cholesterol medication to keep buildup from collecting on the scar and that's what I'm doing now. Lately though, stress is giving me hints as to its power over me but with all the technology and talented surgeons, one of them will probably offer to replace the scarred valve. Will I allow it? I don't know. Maybe not.

The other time I saw my father cry was when his mother died. My grandmother, she was a cute little Indian woman. He took his mother's passing so hard and judging from the way he cried so mournfully I thought he was going to die also. It was scary. He passed out a couple of times. How did the spells happen; he was so strong.

The only other time I remember a doctor other than for myself, was when the family became asphyxiated. I was sitting in a rocking chair in a bedroom with several of the family members and was holding my first born niece in my arms. That was Lupe's first born daughter. I was focused solely on her when I noticed that her eyes started rolling back. I got really scared and started calling for help. Some one! Anyone! No answer! There were about six of us in the house that day. No one was moving.

They were all slumped over! I pivoted and pivoted again. What to do? There was no one to help so either I set the baby down or took her with me. I was in a panic. I don't remember. I ran to the corner meat market and asked the owner to get a doctor and ran back home. I had never heard about a healer for that type of situation. Besides I wasn't thinking clearly, I was just doing the best I could.

The store owners may have had a phone but I don't think so. Nobody else in the neighborhood had one. I don't know what the doctor did but he brought the family back to life. Whether someone called or went for the doctor I'm not sure but it was taken care of. Whew! Thank the lucky stars and our neighbor.

I think what had happened was that at the time the living part of the house had been separated from the kitchen so it was cold. To warm it up my father had built a fire outside and brought some embers nestled in sand in a tub for warmth. Were the embers toxic? Maybe, I was just a kid; I don't know all the facts. I do know that my niece is about eight years younger and she was just a baby then. But eight year old children were considered babies back then, in my culture in that type of situation so I did well. Whew!

Back then some people were much in tune with sensitive forces. It was believed that they could determine or analyze the cause of some diseases or ailments according to bodily signs and symptoms. Not all sensitive persons specialized in all areas. There were different people who specialized in different areas and different levels of expertise. One of our neighbors had looked at my swollen ankle, massaged it carefully and decided it was not sprained and it wasn't. Was it luck, knowledge, or psychic phenomena??? Because from what I hear, revered healers of that nature do have something to offer but they go by different terminology now such as chiropractic, yoga, reike.

One of the ailments that was diagnosed and treated by one neighbor or another was "mal de ojo" which is often misunderstood and loosely translated to *evil eye* but is definitely not in any manner or form witchcraft or voodoo as we know it. People who have not heard about it are often amused when I try to explain our definition of and cure for it. Again, I'll try to explain but please don't quote.

The nearest thing I can compare evil eye with is love at first sight. Now there's a unique occurrence according to me. Well that similar burst of adrenaline at first sight (I think that's what it is) may take place whenever someone with a sensitive or strong aura sees a pretty or interesting something or someone that catches the eye. It may be long beautiful hair on a person, for instance, an interesting beauty mark, a flower on a plant or even just a piece of jewelry that catches the eye and may not even be for any particular reason at all. Even the culprit may not be aware of transmitting the "ojo" because it may happen with just a natural glance at anyone or anything. I only mention a few examples just to give you an idea of a possible adrenaline burst and how it was perceived and handled.

If a person knew or believed that he or she claimed the mentioned aura and it was possible to hurt a person or thing, all they had to do was touch the item and everything would be fine. It only had to be a light touch and nothing else. People who understood or believed the reasoning would readily say yes to a touch. But sometimes it wasn't easy to walk up to a person and ask to be touched or even easy to touch an item or a plant.

Neighbors were aware of who in the neighborhood possessed the aura so they asked around when someone came up with a sudden temperature rise. It seemed that my father was the first one to be asked. It was all good natured. It was all just something that was. Once when he was asked whether he may have given the evil eye to a little boy he said he might have.

It was customary then for children to roam the neighborhood at leisure. The five year old had fallen in a mud puddle after a rainfall and the only clean area was a spot on his belly. The spot was the size of a nickel and just as round. On his way home my father saw him and was tempted to touch the spot but didn't. So he gave the poor kid the evil eye according to the mother. The child was brought over so my father could touch his belly, he did and that was it. It was over.

Thank goodness there was a cure for mal de ojo if it was suspected that an ailing person was afflicted and the source was unknown. For curing purposes the patient rested face up on a bed and the healer with egg in hand prayed while forming small cross symbols all over the body. The egg barely touched the body while being covered with the little crosses. This was done for about ten or fifteen minutes and then the egg without the shell, was placed under the bed in a bowl of water. A little cross from a broom piece of straw or something similar was placed on the water in the bowl. If the illness or discomfort was a result of mal de ojo, an eye was visible on the egg in the bowl after it sat underneath the bed for a little while, if not, it wasn't, and some other home remedy might be performed.

Another ailment.... Once, Jaime came up with a belly ache that could not be cured with istafiate, nutmeg or any other home remedy. One of the neighbors, a local curandero (healer) said my brother may have swallowed a seed and the seed may have attached to the lining of his stomach. He diagnosed it as "empacho" and prescribed a remedy. To cure the ailment he said to place the boy on the bed face down, rub mentholated ointment, salve or something similar on the back and massage for a while. After that the healer could either perform the ritual himself or have a family member perform the task. The person performing the ritual was to grab as much skin as possible with both hands along the boy's mid back and pull and kind of tug as if trying to pick up the boy by his skin. Don't take it wrong but it sort of reminds me of a cat or dog transporting a litter to safety.

I think I remember hearing that there should be some type of "dislodging" indication if you listened carefully so as to know when to stop the tugging. As it turned out my brother was fine soon after the ritual was performed. Do you suppose it was the result of the remedy or was it just that he didn't want to be "tortured" again? What do you think?

Oh, I forgot to tell you this part. When the neighbor was trying to diagnose the stomach ailment he kept talking to himself with his eyes closed as if there was no one else in the room except Jaime. He said something like this in a quiet calm voice, " *Dicen el nino se comio una semilla. Dicen la semilla se quedo en el estomago. Dicen la semilla se esta inflamando*". I don't know where he was hearing this from or whether he was receiving it from his own instincts but he kept talking the whole time. When he was done he prescribed the remedy.

At that time neighbors were as close as family and were always looking out for each other. Everyone helped without even a thought of reciprocation. Most often than not a home cooked meal was exchanged for a favor but it was offered at any time just as a neighborly gesture. There were plates flying all over the barrio. Payment or donation was considered an insult. Are there still similar neighbor somewhere? I wonder.

My mother's contribution for under the weather neighbors was a bowl of hot home made vegetable soup with home made tortillas or her delicious empanadas with a serving of hot cocoa brewed with plenty of stick cinnamon. The smell of the delicacies alone probably perked up the appreciative neighbor.

I need to tell you this one even though it doesn't fall under the same topic but it's interesting. Would you believe that if an underage child or young adult was caught smoking by a respectable adult, and the majority of adults were respectable, that neighbor was thanked for slapping the cigarette out of the smoker's mouth? Also a reprimand on the spot was in order if a child was disrespectful or spoke inappropriate language. It was the adult's responsibility to do so. Can you imagine what would happen now if something like that happened? Slap or reprimand someone, especially a kid? I don't think so!

This is fun so let me tell you about "susto". I don't remember it happening to any of us but I heard it happen to neighbors. If a child lost appetite, wasn't feeling well or looked chalky, which wasn't easy for a brown person, that child had been frightened by something, according to a neighbor's expertise. In that case the child was placed on a bed facing upward and covered from head to toe with a sheet. An adult, usually the mother, took a broom and swept the child from head to toe and then across from hand to hand while repeating a prayer for about fifteen minutes. The prayer was preferably the Apostle's Creed but could be the Our Father. If the child was not better soon a different ritual was performed and could not be performed by just anyone. It had to be administered by someone who knew exactly the way it should be done. Like I said, this never happened to any of us so I have no idea as to what exactly happened or how it was done. All I know is that alum, "piedra alumbre" was needed and at the end of the ritual a sign of the "culprit" would be imprinted on it. Once the source of the fright was evident the child would then be counseled back to a healthy state.

I only saw a "piedra alumbre" once after a ritual had been performed and I was supposed to see a child on a railroad track and a train speeding toward her. I was young at the time and not very interested in such adult beliefs. But that's interesting and sounds like food for thought because, remember, as young kids we did have to cross the railroad tracks to get to school. Trains must have looked huge and scary at such a young age. I don't remember whether I saw the image on the alum but some swore it was there. I don't know what else to say about this. Although, it would be very interesting to hear it from someone who has performed the ritual, knows more about it, or was there to experience the whole thing through. At this point I would really be interested in hearing a knowledgeable, informed person explain the procedure and belief. Wow! That would be awesome!

Not only did we have the ability to take care of unhealthy situations but we also took care of threatening storms. When the sky became too dark for comfort that meant a storm was brewing in the air for sure. In that case one of the neighbors or one of the mothers with a small child would perform a ritual to dissolve the threat. Either a neighbor or a mother would take a young child preferably under five years of age, placed a butcher knife in the child's hand, held it and guided it so as to "cut" the threatening dark clouds with the knife. A cross-like procedure was performed for cutting the clouds. Meteorologists didn't have anything on us did they?

Part 5

Laundry

One of the things I studied when I should have been resting when I was sick but walked around from window to window instead was my mother's laundry routine. Oh my gosh! Our clothes had to be the cleanest and most germ free laundry, anywhere.

Temporarily the laundry routine was altered when we migrated but here is how each routine went when we were home: My mother's routine included a huge black iron kettle of scalding water over a campfire in which she dipped whites after scrubbing them in sudsy water on a scrub board once. Actually the water didn't start out sudsy. It became sudsy with a bar soap my mother used. From the kettle they went back to another sudsy scrubbing, a tub of rinse water and then another rinse tub. If any of the items needed starching, they went into a third prepared tub of starch water, then finally to the clothes line. I don't remember whether colors were dipped in scalding water but the rest of the routine followed the same procedure. The starched clothes went to the clothes line together with the rest of the laundry. After the clothes were dry with the wind swaying them back and forth and the sun helping, all the clothes came down.

Laundry which was to be pressed or ironed whether starched or not were sprinkled with water and formed into a tight bun-like roll. Those were placed in one of the tubs which had been cleaned, rinsed and dried for that purpose. Buns were left overnight to dampen evenly from the sprinkled water and to be ironed the following day. Laundering was a whole day affair and it was about the same for ironing. I don't remember whether my mother came in for lunch. She must have because I'm sure she got hungry. Also, she always prepared at least three meals per day and more often than not an afternoon snack. I guess she came in, cooked, ate, and went out again. By now you know my mother cooked don't you?

I keep taking time out but please don't give up on me. But I need to take time here again to tell you that even though my mother virtually lived in the kitchen she did get routine breaks. On Wednesday evening and one other day of the weekend both parents went to the movies. Movies exhibited at the theaters we frequented were clean with no annoying, embarrassing scenes so they were fun to watch and enjoy with or without the family. My parents made a game of movie day. My father tried to sneak out of the house but my mother was always ready to throw down her apron and join him. Factually, my father would not have gone to the theater without her, when we were home not migrating.

They walked about a mile to the movies. That's probably the reason we had left over fuel vouchers more often than not because we walked wherever we went except to work. I never actually measured the distance as I did, by automobile, from home to my childhood school but it seemed like a mile walk to the theater. My mother was five foot three and her legs were short but that didn't stop her from keeping up with my father who had long legs and was about eight inches taller.

The above game took place in Robstown where we relocated after we left Lyford which had one single theater. There we went to the movies only on weekends. Robstown had three theaters. The nearest one which was about a mile away offered Spanish movies and charged a twenty-five cent entrance fee. Come to think about it I don't even know whether the location can actually be called a theater. It was a huge tent called La Carpa which had a projector and a theater sized screen. The other two which we walked to but my parents didn't were farther. Those were across the street from each other and were exactly one point four miles far, the fee was a little more expensive and didn't offer Spanish movies.

I actually called one of my nieces and asked her to measure the mileage on her automobile odometer. I told her that I wanted my story to be as accurate as possible because the saying states that the older we get, the farther we walked, the more we sacrificed etc. My niece who is a clown and a half and keeps us laughing when we get together gave me some advice. She said it would sound better and more interesting if I said the theaters were five miles away. She followed up with a number of fabricated events and occurrences for me to include. Nope....we walked one point four miles to the theaters.

I'm done with interrupting now: When migrating, my mother laundered some of our work clothes and whites during the week but it was just scrubbing clothes in a tub of sudsy water, rinsed twice, hung to dry, taken down and folded. No scalding water for whites and not much starching. On Sundays, we girls did some of the laundry. We followed my mother's routine with our work clothes - no whites- but laundry included our work bonnets which were called "garsoles" and the detachable cotton-picking straps if we were in the cotton fields, otherwise no straps.

Not everybody who picked cotton used detachable straps. Those were homemade straps basically essential for serious cotton pickers. They were about four inches wide of padded material from old worn cotton sacks and had heavy duty hooks at both ends. The length and the width of the tailored straps depended on the size of the person who would wear it.

The hooks resembled the hooks on overalls. Remember those? Instead of hooking onto buttons though, we used a wad of cotton to secure the strap to the sack after removing the commercially attached strap. The wad served as a button which reminds me of the buttons we covered to match the garments we sewed. It resembles the way the material goes around the metal button to be covered.

I really don't know how my father made the hooks but they were made from really heavy duty metal wire. Commercially attached straps were flimsy single layered straps. Those bunched up and hurt and scratched the shoulder and neck from the weight of the cotton. Also, they didn't endure much weight and easily ripped off of the sack so we had specially made straps.

The bonnets we wore in the fields were basically heavy-duty white rectangles also made from remnants of soft, worn cotton sacks. They had seams running to about half of the length of the rectangle. The seams were about two inches apart in which two inch wide and about a foot long cardboard strips were inserted. The cardboard slats were cut to a length of about two and a half inches from the face so as to shade it. Two tie ends at the back end of those inserts made it a very protective head piece for face, head and nape. Cardboard lengths were removed and tie ends undone for easy laundering. There were two other longer tie ends to secure the bonnet to the head and there were five cardboard sections in all. Bonnets were very practical and comfortable.

While migrating, there was not much ironing to be done. For one, we mainly wore work clothes during the week and the second reason was because we improvised. We opted to wear clothes that did not require ironing if possible because it was difficult to iron with the irons we had at that time. Those irons had detachable handles and were easier to work with at home on the wood burning stove than on the portable kerosene stove. On the kerosene stove we placed the griddle over the flame and placed one iron at a time on it. Believe me that was not an easy task. That took much longer and was more difficult than the wood burning stove routine. Not that the irons on the wood burning stove were easy to work with, mind you, but we did what had to be done.... easier.

I didn't get to iron with the two irons with detachable handles but my two elder sisters did. My mother didn't do much of the ironing after the girls were able to and that was at a young age. Although, I don't think they could have started before the age of eleven because ironing was a serious chore. Those irons were placed on the wood burning stove, handles detached, until they got hot. A handle was then attached to one iron and it was ready for use. When one iron became cold the other one was ready for alternating so as not to break the cycle. After years of wear, however, the handles would sometimes detach themselves from the iron on their own, so the girls had to be extra careful.

Once, Lupe was ironing and the iron came off of the handle and dropped to the floor. My father was in the room and it was the first time he saw it happen. Bang! It startled him and he got up so fast that we didn't even realize what was happening. He went and grabbed the irons, threw them out and left – he always just left when he realized or knew something was needed at home. As usual he wasn't gone too long and on the way back he brought back an iron with a tank attached to it. That was a kerosene iron. That one I did get to use.

At that time we were setting up the ironing board which my father had whittled and fabricated, not directly under but almost under a makeshift alter. Whittling was one of his relaxing pastimes and he created lawn chairs plus other items. The sturdy ironing board was one of them.

The altar was just a few inches above our heads. My mother decorated and replaced homemade crepe paper flowers and streamers often on that corner alter.

One day I was to start ironing but the iron needed kerosene so I went through the procedure of disconnecting and refilling the oil tank. After connecting the tank back on the iron I lit the wick and started to iron. Was it a wick or did it work with something other than a wick? I'm not sure. Whatever the case may be, I lit a match. When I started ironing again I heard a kind of crackling sound and wondered why it was so windy in the house. I thought the breeze was rustling the flowers and streamers on the makeshift alter. But it wasn't that. The sound I heard was my hair crackling! I must have touched my head after I filled the kerosene tank, lit the match and my hair dropped in. I was fine after slapping my head frantically when I realized what had happened. Just a few strands of hair on my head were crinkled, thank goodness. Think about the things we survive in life! What if it had been my dress that became ignited? I had not been introduced to the stop, drop and roll technique yet. I don't remember smelling anything though. I guess I was extra scared because it had to stink. Hair burning…. it had to stink! Pew!

Part 6

Migrating

Before we started migrating we teamed up with another troquero. He was a close friend of my father's. A troquero was a truck owner who transported pickers to and from the fields kept track of their earnings, collected and paid them their share. I think it is safe to say that he was a contractor.

I don't know what kind of arrangement that was between us and the contractor but I suppose he collected contractor stipend. All I know is that the contractor didn't pick cotton; my father did. The contractor was there to place the sacks on the scale, help load the sack on the truck bed for males and load and empty for females. He must have been a true to the fact contractor because on our own we didn't get help for any of that. Girls in the families who migrated with us later did get help at the weigh station.

Also the contractor would be on the lookout. Whenever a female took the sack strap off her shoulder that meant she was ready for the scale so he walked over to carry it to the weigh station. Usually the scale was set up at a very convenient location but sometimes the sacks were full before we got there so he helped carry it.

 After we took off on our own, when the sack was full which was usually eighty to one hundred pounds we grabbed the tie end of the sack, rolled it toward us, draped it over the shoulder while somewhat stooping, stood up and walked to the weigh station with the sack over the shoulder. Once there we slid the scale strap under the sack, hooked up the strap, slid out from under and hooked the sack strap onto the scale hook. We then checked the weight, posted that on a ledger, unhooked the sack, went through the same procedure of getting the sack on the shoulder, walked up the ladder, placed the sack on the truck bed and empted it. When the truck was not full the ladder was a four rung ladder and when it was almost full slats were added and the climb with the sack over the shoulder was longer. If at least two of us got to the scale at the same time the process was easier. The scale was a heavy duty rectangle about four inches wide and about eighteen inches long which hooked onto a sturdy wooden tripod. Unbelievable that we did all that isn't it....huh?

If I hadn't lived that life myself I would say that it was either a lie or that the truth was really stretched. But I was there. I lived it. I really don't know whether that was the norm however. Maybe we were the only ones who did that to that extent. Migrant workers were many but I cannot speak for them. This is my life as I remember it and without exaggeration. And looking back on it now, I wonder how I managed to remain proud, prim and proper in spite of the kind of work we did. I didn't consider myself poor even though we worked in the fields, worked so strenuously, and migrated. Go figure.

When we started migrating we owned a truck whose hood opened from the side. I think it was the norm back then. Under the hood there were a few wires, spark plugs and a battery. An experienced family who learned we were to start migrating warned us about "La Loma de Ferica" as when someone talks about a monster. That was an elevated area in Fredericksburg, Texas territory. Sure enough the first time we traveled that highway the truck was having difficulty climbing so my father got off and started pushing. He pushed either with his back or shoulder until we made it to the top. At one point he got tired and needed a break so he placed a brick right behind one of the truck tires to keep it from rolling backward and just held the truck with the help of the brick. I can't imagine a brick on the roadside. Did he heed the neighbor's warning and was prepared for the slope? Thank goodness the tires on the truck were tiny and the truck was not as heavy as compared to our trucks now otherwise the brick would have been worthless.

The worse thing was that none of us could help. The only one who could have helped was Jaime but he was driving. After my father pushed the truck up the hill his shoulder was never the same but he never saw a doctor. The older he got the more he massaged and rotated his shoulder to try to ease the pain. After the pushing incident we tried to steer away from Fredericksburg until we got the faithful truck which remained with us for the duration of our migrating years. Neither truck left us stranded on the roadside. Not ever. We were lucky.

The way it worked at the beginning was that we started picking cotton in lower south Texas which was home. In time we migrated for different fruits and vegetables in addition to cotton in my father's best interest to keep us fed and clothed as the economy dropped. We traveled for cotton harvest from the lower southeast part of Texas, up north, northeast, west and then to the top of the panhandle. That's located at the uppermost northwestern area of the state. In Levelland, we picked cotton for the same farmer several years in a row. We made some good friends there.

That means we cut across the whole, huge state of Texas and beyond. Hopping from field to field we ended up as far north as the Great Lakes in Michigan. We harvested fruits and vegetables and cultivated fields there and on the way over. Whenever the mileage was more than we could handle we pulled over on the roadside to sleep. We placed canvas sacks on the ground, grabbed a sheet, a blanket and a pillow and that was our bed for the night. Now that I think back on that, it's a miracle we were never bothered by travelers or wildlife. We definitely slept on the roadside on the way back home if not on the way over.

For cotton harvest when we started migrating we traveled northward from where we lived. It was about the only direction we could go. We parked in a town surrounded by cotton fields ready to be harvested where farmers came to pick a truckload of harvesters randomly. Once farmers got to know us they picked us over others. They knew we would do a good quick job. Yes. There was a way of doing a good job. The trick was to pick all cotton off of the vine, pick up any from the ground which wasn't much and retrieve the cotton we dropped if we dropped any. It was easy not to be meticulous but we had been hired to do a job and we were going to do it. That was an unspoken promise from my father. If cotton was left in the field, farmers would lose profit. They wouldn't reap all benefits of their share of labor.

In time it got to the point whereby my father inspected the harvest fields. If he didn't know the farmer or was not familiar with the farmer's cultivating practices the men were escorted to inspect the fields. If my father approved, we picked the cotton, if not we waited for another farmer.

If fields were not cultivated properly or appropriately, too many weeds or wild grass made it difficult to get to the cotton. In that case it wasn't profitable to harvest so we didn't. There were some farmers that my father trusted so there was no need to inspect their fields. He just told them we would be there shortly. One Hispanic family in Granger was one of those he trusted. We became friends with the family and it was understood that we would harvest for them.

My father was a man of few words but his demeanor elicited respect with little effort. (He was so nicely dressed and wore an expensive hat both when he went out and when we traveled.) Farmers who got to know us treated us with respect while under their hire. One thing that really bothered my father, though, was when farmers mispronounced his surname when they greeted him. He was very easy going and patient but when his surname was mispronounced his left temple palpitated. It was subtle, it didn't happen often and he didn't react unfavorably, but when his temple palpitated it was noticeable for those who knew him. He had a way of calming down really fast, however, and in the case where his name was mispronounced he pronounced it correctly and it was over. I didn't blame him for getting upset though. His surname, which is my maiden name, has a beautiful Spanish ring and meaning to it. Anglos, not knowing this, butchered it with what they thought was the English counterpart but no way! There's no comparison. It's a beautiful name with a very distinguished ring to it, I think. I really like it and pronounce it proudly.

At times it was sweltering hot and at other times it was freezing cold mainly when we were in the cotton fields. We always carried a huge wooden barrel at least three quarter full of drinking water in the truck. We drank water with a long handled dipper which hooked onto the barrel. At freezing times like that we had to break the ice that formed at the top of the barrel so we could get a drink of water. We would be sweating but the water was frozen.

We never ate cold food for lunch though. If the field where we were working was close enough my mother delivered a hot lunch for us; if it was far my father built a fire to heat our lunch. He was an expert at that. After lunch we normally took time for a nap. We were in the fields before sunup and left when we couldn't see the cotton by daylight anymore so the nap was very welcomed. We slept under the truck for shade. A fifteen minute nap worked wonders. Dawn to dusk! How about that? We saw the sun come up; we saw the sun go down while in the fields.

Whenever it rained we stopped working, sat in place and covered ourselves with our sacks; if it stopped raining we continued working; if it didn't stop raining, we went home. Those were pleasurable times because sometimes we went to the nearest town after it stopped raining. We didn't pick wet cotton.

We always had fruit at "home" and something to read. I didn't like Gabriela's True Confession magazines so I taught myself to read Spanish. I don't know how I did that but I remember writing the name Rita on the ground when I learned that letters spelled words. Rita must have been one of the characters in one of my mother's novels. Besides, Spanish isn't very difficult once you start putting letter sounds together.

My mother always had Spanish novels on hand – just in case. We got under the covers – on the floor of course – had an apple or another piece of fruit and read. Besides reading material, we also carried embroidery and crochet paraphernalia. Often instead of reading, Gabriela and I embroidered pillow cases which used for decorative purposes when we were home not while migrating. Pillow cases were always white and so were sheets. We carried embroidery needles, an abundance of embroidery stein and iron-on transfers which worked really well on white material. We experimented with different colored steins to create realistic effect. We took a green and a lime strand or two for spring-like greens, for instance, and made brown with orange or yellow for fall color effect. After embroidering we crocheted an edge at the open end. Those pillow cases were ironed and not slept on. We removed them from the pillows for sleeping.

In addition to pillow cases we also embroidered some of the doilies that went on the furniture at home and crocheted a lace-like trim around them. But mostly, doilies were just crocheted without the embroidered center. Crocheted doilies were white thread and crochet hooks were small hook needles so as to create dainty looking doilies. Sometimes we used colored thread for edging the doilies but not too often. By gosh, we were so creative.

I learned a faster way of crocheting from my maternal grandmother. Mostly crochet thread was wrapped around the pinky finger and unwound while crocheting, stop, wind more thread around the finger and continue. Thread was picked up with the hook from between the index finger and thumb.

The way my grandmother taught me was to wrap the thread around the little finger once. Then go under the next two fingers, over the index finger and pick up the thread from the top of it. The pinky worked up and down to feed the thread to allow for continuous crocheting. The index did its own share of work and the method went much faster and smoother.

Rain... What more could I ask for than when it rained? We couldn't do the above type of relaxing on weekends. Often we were in the fields for about six hours on Saturday morning which placed us at about noontime. At that time we went home ate, bathed and got ready to go to the nearest town. My parents would do the main grocery shopping while we roamed the town. That was interesting and fun. Yeah!

Once in a while, the men went to the movies on Sunday afternoons while women and children stayed "home." At one of those times, another family was sharing the house where we were staying. That was a very pretty two story house. It seemed as if it had been owned by another farmer and sold to the new land owner. He owned a similar house not too far from the one we occupied. I wonder whether the depression forced the previous owners out of their land as it also forced us out of ours. Farm foreclosures were not uncommon at the time. As kids we didn't worry about things like that but I think about it now. How sad.

One of the girls in that family who shared the house with us had really long hair which she braided into a long, loose braid at night. On one of those evenings when the men weren't home all the young ladies were on the floor side by side relaxing on blankets, talking and giggling. Suddenly one of the girls let out a really loud scream and we all jumped up. She screamed that there was a snake in the room. We looked everywhere but there was virtually nowhere for the snake to slither without being seen. After a good serious search we relaxed and continued our giggling. Again the same girl screamed and jumped up just in time for me to see that the snake had followed or had attached itself to her when she jumped up. It was hanging from her head! It wasn't a snake.

It was her braid! The whole thing was hilarious. We laughed that night until our sides ached and for a long time after that when we remembered the "snake".

That there was a snake in the room was not illogical because such houses were vacant for long periods of time. They offered free lodging for all kinds of critters. Once we stayed at a house where there were centipedes among other crawly creatures. One crawled up my aunt's back under her shirt. She felt the centipede and grabbed it away from her body with her shirt. She was terrified speechless and kept pointing at the hand on her back which held the centipede. Those things were huge! How someone managed to decode her pantomime and help her out of her shirt or how they got the centipede, is beyond me. I don't remember whether the men were home that evening or not. Maybe not because the one thing I remember is a lot of hand flapping, oohing and pivoting not knowing what to do.

My father had two brothers who migrated with us a couple of times. They also drove well maintained automobiles at the time. They were both married. One of the brothers and his wife had no children. His wife was the one with the centipede. After about thirteen years of marriage they adopted a baby boy. The baby was tiny and fit in a lady's shoe box. Very soon after they adopted, they had a son. This one wasn't tiny at all. The other couple had one child, Ana, whom they dressed nicely and was allowed to spend time in the field with her dad and rode on his cotton picking sack. Her mother also went to the fields whenever she had time to spare. At times Ana got off of her father's sack, picked cotton and placed it in piles for her parents to pick up as they went by.

On another one of those Sundays when we were home without the men, we decided to sit outside for a while. It was twilight and the men would be home soon. The truck lantern-like beams would be on and we would spot them coming down the road. Well, before the truck came treading down the road, we spotted a car which stopped about a couple of miles away. The lights to the car were turned off but we could see the silhouette sitting there. Everyone got scared, went indoors and turned off any lantern or lamp that was lit and walked out into the night again to enjoy the cool breeze. The car didn't move. Once in a while a little light flicked and we knew the car was still there. The mothers decided the occupants were probably planning an attack so they went indoors, pulled out pots and pans, filled them with water and lit a fire under them. Kids huddled. We waited. We whispered. But the ladies stood ready to counterattack with that boiling water! No one was going to mess with us! Tell me that that wasn't an ingenious military counterattack. I thought it was. The men got home before anything happened....bummer. We were ready for war!

On some Sunday evenings whether the men were home or not all the ladies just clustered and relaxed around my mother around a flickering lamp light as she narrated a novel she had read or the one she was reading at the time. Either way, at curfew, the narration would be placed on hold until the next time we could sit for continuation. There were, of course, a lot of aah's when we had to stop. Aah?!

Another time we stayed at a little house which was in the center of brambles and thorns. Only a small area had been chopped down all around the house. That was rabbit territory and they weren't afraid to come right up to the door and sit on their hinds to greet us at any time. They were so cute and friendly, yet we ate them.

My father owned a very old rifle that he always carried - very well hidden- when we traveled. No one was allowed to touch that rifle except for that one time with the rabbits to provide some of our meals. At dusk when we came home from the fields the boys took turns shooting at the multitude of rabbits. It was no contest. Bullets couldn't miss the poor little friendly rabbits even if they tried.

As I've mentioned before, my mother was a very good cook so we didn't mind having rabbit for lunch and supper for the duration of that job. My mother worked wonders with spices which she ground on a "molcajete" (grinding bowl). The grinding bowl was made of speckled stone and stood on three "knobs". For grinding the spices or hot sauce peppers there was a pear shaped grinding tool. With the help of those spices and my mother's expertise, the rabbit feasts we had were cooked several different forms and were very tasty. At that time there was another family migrating with us. It was the mother, two young ladies and a young man. He and Jaime supplied the rabbits for many of our meals for the duration of our stay there.

My mother believed that cooked rabbit would not taste gamey if she removed what she called "el monte" from just above the rabbit's foot. I think that's where she said it was. She said it was a wad-like bitter mass which accumulated or collected in that particular area. (To me, that sounds like an appendix.) When removed, there was no bitter, gamey or aftertaste in the cooked meat. Whether it was that or her cooking talent, I'm not sure. All I know is that the food was delicious and satisfying after a long day's work.

My father was very proud of the aforementioned rifle. He kept it well cleaned and oiled. But that was the only other time I had seen the rifle fired. The first time was when he shot our dog. I really liked that dog. It was a collie and I was just a little taller above his head whenever I put my arm around his neck. One day we heard a really loud, painful whimpering and simultaneous growling, groaning coming from down the road. It was our dog!
We were told to hurry inside and from the tone of my father's voice we knew he meant business so we scurried. He, himself, went in, found the rifle and waited at the door. We watched and waited by a window. The dog was swaying everywhere, something awful and growled and bared his teeth. I had never seen him like that before. He didn't look like my dog at all. As soon as he was in shot range, my father shot him and the dog went down. I can still visualize that scene when I recall the incident. Sigh. But then I recall pleasant memories of my arm around his neck and I feel better. My poor dog, he was so soft and pretty.

That rifle remained with us for many years before my father finally passed it down to the elder son-in-law. According to my father he had gotten it in 1914 during the revolution. It seemed that Pablo, who really admired the rifle, would be the one to appreciate the priceless and sentimental value of it so he received it as a gift in either the late sixties or early seventies. My brother-in-law together with the family owned a dairy farm too far from firefighter help so their house burned down to the ground and the fire destroyed the valued rifle.

Often I missed my dog and thought about him at times as I walked leisurely through the fields. In a field somewhere during one of my walks I was distracted as I came across a stash of Indian arrowheads. Some looked like they were ready for use and others were at different stages of whittling. I studied them, played with them and admired them but didn't save any. If I did I lost them later. I don't think I ever told anyone. I had no idea those arrowheads were or could become priceless. Yes, about arrowheads, I would have probably learned in school and known they were valuable artifacts had I attended full-time sessions but then I wouldn't have been in the field to see them…. right? Humor me please.

Once we even stayed at a place which was walking distance from an ocean. I have no idea how that happened. While there I learned to swim because I went in the water every night. Toward the end of our stay, however, we were warned to stay out of the water because sharks had been spotted too close to the beach. Bummer.... that was the only opportunity I ever had for swimming so eventually I forgot how to swim. At this point I would drown in two feet of water if I jump in. I'm sure.

In one of the cotton fields we were attacked by an interesting, traveling tumble weed which rammed right into us but it turned out to be friendly. Some of us were at the weigh station when it hit. It was a big one. It had a well secured note attached to it which asked to please say where we found it and set it on its way again. It had already traveled almost two hundred miles when we found it. We added the new information and placed it out in the open to continue its journey. I wonder how much farther it traveled. Out in the open, the weeds flipped, turned and sometimes traveled faster than our old truck did. They glided, bounced and danced gracefully as the wind helped them along on their journey. It was such a delight to watch them travel.

Another time while in a field I was minding my own business just picking cotton and all of a sudden I did a quick breath intake and froze. In a second my father was there with a stripped-down branch of cotton plant and killed a snake right in front of me. That was scary!

My father always tried looking out for us and tried to protect us. Now I wonder whether he felt guilty for not giving us a better life or a better education. I thought we had a good life. (Once I mentioned that to a white acquaintance and was told it was because I didn't know anything else. Ouch! Double Ouch!)

If my father's concern was about schooling many kids dropped out of school at a very early age whether they were migrants or not. But he believed in education. Both my parents were literate – mostly in Spanish – but literate. I don't know how they got their education. Both grandfathers died at a very early age. My maternal grandmother continued minding a small store which was located at the front of her home. My paternal grandmother together with her kids continued working and maintaining a small livestock farm for a while until it was decided to relocate. That leads me to believe that it wasn't easy for either of my parent to become educated. It must have been just as difficult for them to become educated as it was for us. They didn't talk much about it but neither did we about ours.

One of the things I remember about my father other than a keen intelligence was his love of classical music. Once we started listening to our own music he wondered how we could call it music. I wonder what he would think of the music young people listen to now. We had a crank-up, upright beautiful shiny Victrola turn table and listened to a great collection of music, beautiful music. That record player was left behind when we moved to Robstown. There was no room in the truck to transport it and we never went back for it. Records were fragile thirty-threes and later forty-fives. I think that meant revolutions per minute.

It was evident that my father had a healthy level of education. He spoke English and spoke it well but only utilized it when it was necessary. The difference between my father and my mother in this area is that she had no need or desire to speak English. They were both educated so surely they wanted or needed us to have the opportunity of formal education.

Unfortunately they had much more to worry or be concerned about other than a degree of guilt or our education. Obviously migrating offered very legitimate concerns not only while we dwelt in abandoned houses or in the fields but also as we traveled. There had to be a generous degree of apprehension, fear and worry. At times we were totally exposed, defenseless and vulnerable in the middle of nowhere as we slept on the roadside. We kids slept peacefully and woke up refreshed but I'm sure my parents didn't. How could they?

For us it was exciting and fun because we walked around and explored after we had sandwiches or tortilla wraps. After that we slept on our makeshift beds and counted stars until we dropped off one by one. We were relaxed and content, even happy but my parents had to be aware that we were sure prey for predators and/or plunderers. Wow! Did they ever sleep? I get chills now just thinking about it. I'm glad I didn't think about all that when I was young and on the road. My parents didn't instill fear in us though. They didn't say don't do this or that nor don't go here or there so we weren't afraid at all. But I bet they were.

I may not remember exactly what we harvested where other than when we harvested cotton, nonetheless, eclectic experiences and memories are etched in my memory as we traveled outside of Texas while migrating. Aside from the beautiful terrain and some not so beautiful, there were so many different sights and events to experience. We saw quaint little towns and buildings, cute little old churches, some with traditional steeples which could be seen from miles away. Those were very awesome to spot during our extended hauls.

long hauls.

There was one steeple in particular that I remember but that was in Texas. It seemed to be located all by itself among nothing but trees and when we were at a certain distance it seemed like it was on the road and we would run right into it. Also there was a night light aimed right at the steeple. That light made the area around the church appear heavenly. It was so awesome that one of the men who migrated with us together with his family couldn't look at it. It scared him. For me it was fascinating and mesmerizing. It was beautiful. Awesome!

It became a totally different experience when we started migrating out of Texas. There were mountains in Texas but it was nothing as compared to mountains in other states we visited. The first time we drove to Colorado, for instance, we traveled and traveled endlessly. At one point there was nothing but mountains and that was scary. It seemed as if we would dead-end at the bottom of mountains which lined a never-ending horizon. I just knew we would have to turn right back once we couldn't go forward. That was it. And I surely wasn't looking forward to the long, long drive back to civilization.

Then suddenly towns, life and fields started popping out of nowhere. Life! Great! What a relief! I finally remembered to breathe and did. After I turned un-blue I enjoyed the never-forgotten, beautiful terrain and interesting sights. Once I relaxed, I surmised we would work, enjoy and at the end take a relaxed journey back home. We did. Ahh!

When traveling out of Texas I recall that we harvested cherries, apples and cucumbers around the Great Lakes and other crops on the way there. When I say around it doesn't mean we could touch the water, it just means we were about twenty or thirty miles away. Other crops I remember harvesting is spinach, green beans, carrots and onion seed. We harvested tomatoes in Ohio. That I remember because the house in which we stayed was surrounded by a huge area of beautiful lawn-like grass. It resembled Bermuda grass because it was close to the ground but there was no visible seed as in Bermuda.

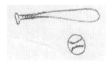

The turf was perfect for playing softball and we played every chance we got. Another family on Pablo's side of the family was also in the area so we had enough players for games. When we didn't have enough players I would hit fly balls. I had practiced and trained myself to hit the ball really hard with the bat because I wasn't a fast runner. So when I played with the school team I was prepared to try for homeruns and I became proficient at that. Hitting fly balls was fun but I was partial to games. And you thought I was perfect, huh.

Well I couldn't run. I was really slow as compared to my team mates.

One thing we didn't harvest but cultivated around the Great Lakes area was sugar beets. For that we worked with a short handled hoe. I think the purpose of the short handled hoe was so we could be close to the ground and see the sprouting plants better. Our job was to leave only one sprout per space and leave a certain amount of space between each plant. Sometimes clustered sprouts were very close together and could not be separated with the hoe. We had to pluck those by hand until only one sprout was left behind. Now there I didn't fare as well as my siblings and my father. It really mattered because we were paid by the acre. I came close to tape measuring the distance between plants and glass magnifying to assure that only single sprouts remained. I peered at those plants as if my life depended on it. Can you believe that?!

Once we also stacked I don't know what or I should rather say that we up righted something that resembled corn stalk but it wasn't that. We up righted the stalks in the shape of Indian teepees but that's all I can say about that. I do remember however, that one of my knees hurt while we were there but it didn't last so I didn't say anything. I had never experienced pain like that before so it must have been the early start of my rheumatic fever syndrome. Bummer, not me?

As I write I thank goodness, thank luck, the stars and mention fortunate as if there was no other force working for us but surely there had to be a Higher Power on our side. A Higher Power listening to and taking care of us because of my mother's constant praying. Otherwise how else did we survive without incident throughout our migrating years and other efforts?

We never suffered from sprained or broken bones and that was a miracle considering our line of work. We never even suffered a serious virus, pneumonia or bites or stings. We were in danger almost constantly. There's no way I could mention it all. The narrative would be voluminous. But there was danger when we were in the fields, different temporary isolated dwellings, as we traveled and more. It wasn't evident to me then but I see it now. I also mention possible danger zones such as working in freezing weather to say the least as well as in elevated temperatures but I need to communicate that dwellings never had indoor plumbing or even an outhouse. We utilized the best surroundings available as "facilities". Also, breaks while traveling were out in the wilderness where we were totally vulnerable to all types of dangers but I don't even recall a tick incident.

For traveling breaks we would spread out into the wilderness where men and boys went to one side of the road, usually across the road. Women and children went to the opposite side. So how did we survive that plus other threatening perils and dangers? I tell you. There had to be a Higher Power listening to my mother's prayers and looking out for us day and night year after year during our fateful way of life and beyond. We were fortunate in that prayers were heard and supplications answered. What else?

Part 7

Bias Decoding

I didn't think much of the National economy or opinions made against us without adequate basis but slurs were abundant and came in different forms and different areas of our existence. I lived in a prejudiced era when the trend dictated that if you were not white pigmented, you were not an "American"; double jeopardy if you were a migrant; and triple if you were poor. If you were an emigrant, not to be confused with migrant, but white or of pale pigment you were an American no matter how far you traveled from the Native country to get to the United States. I'm sure not all whites qualified as Americans just as I'm sure not all browns were Mexicans. The fact that I am brown placed me in a Mexican, wetback and/or Chicano category. Chicano to me sounded more like "white trash" so we didn't identify with it. But it still served as another blow we really didn't need. I was born and bred in the United States of America, didn't get wet crossing any ocean or river as some "Americans" did but I'm brown and therefore, assumed Mexican. When you figure that one out please let me know.

I cannot legally say however, that our family lived in poverty although we may have hit a low at one point. But I don't remember wearing rags or not having soap for laundry or bathing. We were not concerned with un-American labels either. The fact that we were so involved in our adopted or adapted way of life offered financial security and left no time or need for prejudiced practices. Over and above, my father possessed a knack for instilling in me a very healthy level of pride that facilitated bias-decoding and see it for what it was. He did that without demeaning "Americans". I would have said: Ignorance breeds bigotry but I'm not my father. He believed that in spite of circumstances, slurs and labels whether verbal or written, we possessed a high level of intelligence, were not poverty stricken, nor below the white race as perceived by them. Anglos couldn't see that but there was no reason to fret. The logic was to acknowledge that migrating, color of skin and socio-economic level does not define an individual or a race and let it go at that but at times it was easier said than done. We became upset. We're human.

Once in our travels we ended up at a pavilion-like building where food was being served and learned that people were eating there without paying. We could have eaten there but my father wouldn't hear of it. I didn't know then what it was about but I do now. People were going hungry; we weren't. They needed to eat there; we had food.

I had never seen a bread line or soup kitchen before so we weren't as poor as others. Therefore the poor label attached to us wasn't justified. How dare they? Between my two parents and with our help we were kept clothed, fed and biasing impermeable. Impermeable? Well, I wouldn't attest to that.

But you know what? I really wanted to mingle at the pavilion. It looked like fun because people took their food out to eat at park benches. That reminded me of farm life so I wanted to eat there but my father said definitely no. It would have been fun to mingle.

Our attire was not elegant but it was up to par as compared to our intermittent sphere. My father made sure we dressed in new department store or professionally sewn attire for school. Luckily we had a professional seamstress living right across the ally. My mother helped with material selection. On the way back from migrating we stopped in San Antonio at a department store which offered a wide variety of ready wear. There we could find most essentials for the family. The stores at home were not equipped for that but we did offer support.

To help out with clothing my mother collected same pattern, cotton-print flour sacks to make the dresses we changed into right after we got home from school. That means we did go down with the economy but I'm sure browns weren't the only ones. The "elite" didn't know about the flour sack dresses because they never came to or even looked at our side of town. I guess the "poor" label was attached mainly because we worked in the fields because I don't think white kids had an extended wardrobe either. The change of clothing routine was the norm for most of us who lived in the neighborhood but I don't know whether white students went through the same routine. For a while I wore the same school dress Monday and Tuesday and a different dress on Wednesday, Thursday and Friday unless it didn't look fresh enough for school. I did that until we started working in the fields and got better after I started receiving a weekly allowance while migrating.

Gabriela couldn't stand the home made dresses my mother sewed. They weren't pretty at all. First off my mother was not a seamstress and with everything else she had to do there was no time to be meticulous. The dresses were basically rectangles with holes for head and arms. Those were just wear-at-home dresses but my sister detested them. I didn't mind them but that was because I didn't get to wear them for a long length of time. Also, I was six years younger and my little friends lived in the immediate area, hers didn't so she roamed the neighborhood in her "ugly" dresses.

It may be that at some point she may have worn homemade dresses to school as the economy dropped but I hope not. She was six years my senior so we never attended the same school. She didn't walk to school with the younger kids either so I don't remember whether she wore homemade dresses to school or not. I did see an impressive progression as she got older and after receiving a weekly allowance. I also remember that after she graduated and started working she dressed and carried herself really well, poor or not. Good for her.

At the time we started receiving an allowance for a half day's work it seemed like the economy was picking up. I think it became less worrisome for my parents. My father didn't believe in paying rent and didn't believe in prolonging mortgage payments either. Maybe it came from a lesson learned with the farm. I don't know whether we were making payments. If so, that must have been totally devastating. It bothered him that for about a year or two after we moved to Robstown we leased a residence before we owned our own home again but continued migrating. That's about the time

Gabriela and I started doing things together. Not only did we buy some of our own clothes but we started sewing to stretch our dollars. One of the first blouses I purchased was a very pretty ruffled blouse and my teacher had one just like mine - color and all. I saw her wear her blouse once during the academic year before I wore mine. Chagrin maybe?

Part 8

Migrating Did Not Equate to Ignorance

Previously I said that slurs didn't concern me and that I took discrimination in stride or that I ignored it. I think my nose grew and I like my nose so I'll mention a little something about that here. I was bothered; I'm human. Therefore while I was writing I realized that I wasn't totally as immune as I presumed or believed to be.

I really don't want this manuscript to mirror prejudice or sound negative because that's not what it's about but it goes with the territory. With that in mind, I will only touch on the subject: I couldn't tell you exactly when or where I saw a sign at a restaurant, when migrating, that read: NO MEXICANS OR DOGS ALOUD. No it's not a typo. That's how the sign was written. Maybe you remember signs similar to this. They weren't scarce. Like I said, we ate well we never left the house without having a good meal and had sandwiches while we were out so I had no desire to walk into a dining establishment. But signs had to have bothered me more than I thought or dared to admit because I remember thinking very sarcastically: Who cares?! But please tell me, do you mean that I may walk in, take my well trained pet in with me and sit quietly? I did say slurs didn't concern me and I really wasn't hungry so what was it ....sour grapes?

Much later I saw a sign at a department store that said "HALE" I figured it had to be a Spanish word because it didn't make sense to me in English. I was curious. HALE could mean "Flap your wings" but for it to mean that no matter how far fetched it really needed another E at the end.... HALEE. Then it could possibly mean 'Flap your wings'. Did it really mean flap your wings according to the creator? Judging from that era anything was possible. Yet, it couldn't be. I decided it was meant to encode PULL, if I gave the silent h a j sound. I concluded that that's what the scribe wanted it to say.

Long story short, I went in; asked an employee what the sign meant; overly proud and friendly said it meant pull. I didn't tell her all about my mental hypothesizing but I did tell her the sign didn't really spell a word. Her demeanor changed drastically and she said it had to be correct because it came from the office, so there. So there is mine. The sign was removed even though it came from the office.

Degrading signs I saw throughout my childhood and into my teens. I couldn't tell you exactly when I saw the above one but it could have been during my early to mid teens. I really didn't pay much attention to the abundance of signs before that. Usually signs just read WHITES ONLY or NO MEXICANS so there was no question about it. Whites didn't want to have anything to do with us. They didn't want us around and that was fine with me. However, some restaurants allowed "Mexicans" to pick up a plate to go at the back door and/or were allowed to dine in the kitchen area. I guess if hunger reigned a meal there would be appreciated. But think about it. The "Mexican" was not allowed to sit in the "American" dining area yet was allowed to sit where food was prepared??! What's up with that? Was it that they just didn't want to see our brown pigment? I'll give them that. But that brings up another question. Why all the sun bathing and artificial tanning then? Problemas, Problemas.

About the Pull sign, I'm not sure where I saw the first one but much later I saw another at one of the shopping malls in Corpus Christi and that was in 2006. It was on the door of a very popular chain store. HALE. I just went in and told customer service at the register that it wasn't a word. She said it meant PULL and I left it at that. The sign which came from the main office came down anyway. I don't know how long that sign had been there because that's the only time I have entered that particular store from the outside of the mall. The next time I was there the sign was gone.

Needless to say, it stands to reason that because of such signs, because our language was not accepted and because of verbal and written slurs, racism has hurt my culture more than the Great Depression ever did but I'll elaborate later. Much has been lost in an attempt to blend with the "norm" whatever that is, not to be ridiculed and even at this late date racism is still around especially in my age group. One popular remark is "Go home." The problem is that I have nowhere to go. I'm home. Even my migrating days are over so altogether, I'm home, I'm retired and living peacefully. Thank goodness.

But let me tell you, even though some harbored negative feelings for no apparent reason and outright displayed them, there was a different side to migrating that they didn't know about. Migrating definitely did not equate to ignorance nor did it define poverty or anything negative as often perceived by the "elite" society who scorned us. In fact it offered its own merits and offered learning experiences and opportunities not only setbacks.

We kids were not receiving traditional or formal education in a classroom setting but becoming educated was inevitable in our travels and work experiences. Traveling was educational because of the beautiful and interesting sights and sceneries and there were signs and advertisements to be read. And again, we didn't have the little handheld game or those little movie computers that came in later to distract learning while on the road.

While traveling, I learned to read a map at a very young age and that transitioned to other practical skills. I learned all kinds of math – arithmetic – primarily for problem solving requirements in the classroom and for wage purposes but ultimately for vital purposes. I learned, when we were on the road for instance, how many electric poles equaled one mile, more or less, to figure the mileage to the next town. Wait. I didn't say that correctly. Did I? After learning the mileage to the next town I grouped an amount of poles for each mile to figure how many more groups of poles were needed to get there. Never mind! It made sense to me at the time.

The point is that word problems didn't stunt me as much as they would have if I hadn't created my own little try-not-to-be-bored-on-isolated-road problems while riding in the truck with the wind in my face. I think the first truck we owned ran only about thirty or thirty-five miles per hour so the wind felt good and relaxing on my face. Anyway, acquired computation skills came in handy not only when deciphering word problems in our part time schooling and while migrating but came in handy later in life for survival purposes also. You can be sure of that.

One other educational experience that came in handy when migrating was calculating my allowance. My weekly allowance was however much cotton I picked either Friday after lunch or Saturday morning whichever half day we worked at the end of the week. To figure my allowance I needed to add the amount of pounds of cotton I picked and multiply the poundage by the cash paid per pound at the given time. I presented my calculation to my father and received my allowance for the week. It was a very generous weekly allowance.

Cash per pound didn't fluctuate often or drastically during the harvest year but sometimes it did so I had to keep that in mind. Another calculating requirement was to keep track of and add all pounds picked for the day by each member of the family. At the end of the day one of us added all poundage picked to determine whether the truck was ready for the gin. Does all that sound like ignorance?

Over and above calculating requirements on the field I learned that it was more economical to sew than to purchase ready made clothing. From a pattern, Gabriela and I learned everything we needed to know to make some of our own clothes. That came from our allowance. After we started sewing we carried our paddle sewing machine when we traveled. With all the different and practical areas going on, talk about a math whiz in the classroom! Math also contributed to other vitals in life which may seem non-mathematic but actually are. All that calculating paid off really well in the long run. That was education and no one could take that away from us....Mexicans or not; poor or not.

Part 9

Empty Nest Syndrome

When we were in Lyford I worked at the department store whenever they needed me. There I helped customers with their selections and kept items orderly. Later I also worked at a little convenient store where I manned the register. The owners had a little room at the back of the store where they spent most of their time while I was under their hire. My thought was that now that I no longer attended classes I could work more hours since I had more time to spare. I don't know where I got the idea that I needed to work when we were not in the fields. My father didn't ask me to, I just did. Maybe it's just because I "landed" my first position at a very young age because one of my classmate's parents owned the department store. I was about eleven or twelve at the time. I visited when we were home and that's how I got my first "job". After that I just continued to work. It helped that for many years after I started working an application was not required. Someone needed help; you were hired. Trust was one thing we didn't doubt.

We left Lyford and moved to Robstown which was a town surrounded with more agriculture than our little town had to offer. There I worked at a store when not in the fields. Mostly I stacked groceries and dusted but I bagged groceries also. The owners didn't think I was old enough to handle a register. I was under sixteen years of age and the store was too big. It was too much responsibility for the kid they thought I was. Actually, I really was a kid but I did have register experience so I was promoted to the soda fountain within the store and it didn't take long for that to happen. Yeah....I was promoted!

I worked in the fields, worked at the store when we were not migrating then a taco stand until I finally landed a well-paying full-time position at a hamburger stand. I took home thirty-two dollars and fifty cents per week! Much, much less than picking cotton or fruits and vegetables but we were not migrating as much anymore. Miguel had gone military, Lupe had gotten married and Gabriela had gotten a full time job at a chain drug store. The young kids had to attend school wherever we were so there was not a whole lot of manpower left. The only sibling who was left that could migrate and work was Jaime.

After Miguel came back from the service he married a local girl. His wife Consuelo became a member of our family like nobody I have ever known and was like a daughter to my parents and a sister to us. That made it very easy for my brother to remain faithful to our parents' needs. When my parents, my youngest sister and two brothers ended up in Arizona Miguel left his job, followed them and catered to our parents' needs until the very end. He, himself, left this world shortly after my mother did. Three weeks later to be exact. My father went to a home when Miguel became ill. Beatriz couldn't take over because she had married, had a baby, became widowed in her late twenties, needed to work and we weren't in the area to help. Becoming separated was typical of many migrating families and it wasn't easy to remain close to relatives geographically but we try to stay in touch.

Recently I acquired a picture of Miguel and Connie together with most of the wedding party and that's a good deal. I lost my original one during one of our famous storms. I also lost Lupe's and Pablo's wedding picture and all I have now is a computer copy but that's alright. They were the only two plus one other sibling who had a traditional wedding but I couldn't make it to the third one. That was Flor. I was already married and we were military at that time.

Lupe married at sixteen or seventeen so basically she wasn't part of the migrating family for too long. During that time we were a close knit family and were mostly in the fields. The reason her future husband found her was because cotton picking started at home. There, when people wanted or needed to work they hitched a ride with a "troquero". My father didn't encourage riders because too often it was just kids who went along for the ride or just wanted movie money. My future brother-in-law Pablo hitched a ride with us and that's how he met Lupe. I think. He was very proud of his singing voice so he sang in the field and serenaded her off the field, kind of. He didn't want to get her in trouble so he didn't serenade right at her window which would have been the romantic thing to do. Or maybe it was before he asked for her hand in marriage and didn't make it obvious that he was serenading. Again, who knows? They weren't even allowed to talk to each other in the field let alone anywhere else. In fact, none of us were allowed to talk to boys. I have no idea how they knew they wanted to be married. Did he even ask her or did he just ask for her hand in marriage and hoped for the best? I don't know. All I know is that however it came about they had a very nice wedding.

I was about five years of age at the time, too young to understand much of what went on. All I know is that I was very proud when they married because that was our wedding celebration and I got to sit in the "white" chair when my sister was not in it. The chair was an arm sofa chair which had been covered with a white sheet and placed under a big tent in our back yard. I thought my sister looked very pretty in her white wedding gown. So did Consuelo when she and my brother married. That wedding I don't remember as much about as my sister's. Maybe that's because it was held at her house, naturally, so it's not as vivid. But I do remember that members of the wedding party were beautifully dressed and how handsome my brother looked alongside his beautiful bride in her white wedding gown. Both weddings were very impressive by standards.

The second male in line, Jaime, did most of the driving throughout our migrating years. He was really young when he first took over. He may have been about fifteen and driving without a license but that wasn't uncommon. That was a lot of responsibility for a teen because aside from cotton harvesting, he transported the family plus the picked cotton to the gin.

Transporting the family was a chore in itself because of the amount of traveling we did. He became an avid, trustworthy driver within both driving responsibilities so we really trusted him to get us where we needed to be. Transporting the cotton to the gin, however, may have resulted in a downfall for him in the long run. You see, there was no way for my father to know how much time he actually spent on the job while he was out. That depended on the amount of cotton bales ahead of him to be ginned before his turn came up.

My father was very strict on the field with us but there was no way he could keep track of Jaime's work ethics while he was away. And he had to leave. At times he left to the gin during the day and sometimes in the early evening. It all depended on the time when the truck was full and the required amount needed per bale was loaded on it. That's interesting because maybe he took time out to roam the streets after the truck was unloaded while the rest of us really had to remain on task. If we didn't my father had a shrill type of whistling which he used if he thought we were goofing off on the field. That whistle gave me chills, it pierced through my body.

To whistle he kind of wrapped his lips around his teeth, kind of formed a u with his tongue and blew. I could never do that no matter how I tried. It's not that he watched us constantly or that he was a slave driver but we were to remain on task. I really don't know how to explain it because when we were at leisure, we were at leisure. We were not expected to perform chores wash dishes or cook--ever. Other than while migrating and laundered a few of our work clothes we weren't expected to help with laundry or cleaning when we were home unless we chose to. Our leisure time was relax time. In order to help my mother, Lupe and Gabriela volunteered to do all the ironing when they became responsible enough to iron. They also started helping with housework. I started helping but the girls were meticulous so they didn't allow me to iron or clean as much as they did. Bummer!

Flor preferred to spend time in the yard when we were home. That was her hobby. It paid off because her yard was covered with beautiful grass, lovely plants and flowers after she got her own home. I guess spending time in the yard all those years really paid off. It's amazing how she didn't bother with annuals yet had beautiful flowers blooming year round. How talented.

Another thing that amazes me is not remembering what Beatriz did all those years with the family. She was never underfoot. We didn't ignore her we just didn't see her. Once I asked her where she was all those years but she said she didn't remember. I believed her so forgot about it for a while. Somehow even without sibling help or interference she turned out to be a well rounded person anyway so that was fine. She stuck with us and experienced the same turns of life we did but where was she? Once we started looking at her many, many years later we learned she's a person to be proud of as is the rest of the family. Come to think of it, maybe she was the one who ignored the whole bunch of us. That's amusing....huh?

After I started writing I called and asked her again what she was doing all those years we didn't see her. I had to say something about her. Again, she said she didn't remember but shortly after she called to confess. She said that when she was younger she tried to blend into the family hustle and bustle. When she got older and saw that she could be called on to do chores she sneaked out quietly. She definitely disappeared when she saw a tubful of rolled up "buns" to be ironed and would be asked to help.

And now she wants to know who will play her character when my story is selected for a movie! Maybe I'll leave her out altogether. It's payback time. Now that I think about it maybe that's the reason Flor worked so diligently outdoors. It was better than ironing. Was she really working in the yard? By gosh, they were the two smartest ones in the whole bunch! How rude!

When I told one of my girls about the ingenious youngest sister she suggested that for the movie we show her back as she walks out the door at the start of the movie. Then at the end show her coming back in. We have had so much fun with the imaginary scene. Even the invisible one has gotten a good laugh over it.

Don't tell her this, but my daughter had suggested we show her going in and then out of a closet for the movie. I had to remind her that we didn't have closets back then. We had a rod at a corner of the bedrooms to hang clothes. Too bad, it was such a good idea. I wonder whether everybody knows we didn't have closets. Hmm? Could we get away with the closet idea? Possibly not.

The youngest brother, Antonio, married, had seven kids and we lost track of him for many, many years. After he got tired of roaming he ended up in Arizona. He's there for now. But who knows what he'll do next. He, himself, probably doesn't know what he'll do.

An interesting episode of recalling is that when there were six migrating siblings left only Gabriela and I worked commercially. The three younger ones attended school but what happened to the elder brother of the six, Jaime? And come to think about it, both boys dropped out of school at an early age so what were they doing while we worked and the young girls went to school? I was too busy working to notice.

Jaime may have been stunted because of so much responsibility at such a young age. For him, at that age, what did he do? He was completely under the wing one minute and completely out of the roost the next when migrating. Under, out. Under, out. On top of that he didn't have the responsibility of attending school so he missed out on both discipline and education. How unfortunate.

Now that I think about it I wonder whether he got scared at times when he had to drive back at night all by himself from the gin. When he left late, night had to close in on him. I hadn't thought about that before. Too often roads were isolated between there and where we were staying. He was too young to be out at night on his own. It must have been scary. For that, for all the responsibility and for not scoring as well as expected after migrating we have to blame the depression. He had potential and a very good head on his shoulders.

Jaime, Gabriela and I were the ones hit the hardest by the depression uprooting. Flor got the tail end of it. She did get some tough years, however. She was stronger than I was and worked just as hard as I did for the duration of the migrating years except for short spurts when she attended school while migrating. It was not as tough for the two younger ones. I'm not saying it was easy because it wasn't; it was just not as tough for as long a period of time. Beatriz continued working in the fields but the family was no longer migrating as much.

They had settled in Arizona because harvest in different crops was available year round. Ultimately the depression and migrating was the reason we as a family ended up so far apart geographically. Even faithful visits to close relatives became a rarity after that. How unfortunate.

Part 10

Misnomer

Because racism is not steadfast but still exists in my generation I will give you one incident as an example. I will tell you about the conversation with the white acquaintance at a restaurant. That happened in 2006. I mentioned something about it before so now I have to tell you.

I was having a leisurely lunch with acquaintances whereby one of them had lived in the area all his life and had seen the city grow and farm life diminish. He was very knowledgeable and interesting on the subject. He knew who had inherited from whom how and different transactions which led to where we are now in this area…..more town area, less farm. I listened.

Somehow the conversation ended up in my court so I talked about farming as I know it since that was the topic of conversation. That led into having to leave the farm at a young age and to migrating experiences which brought me to this geographical area to stay. I talked about how I had enjoyed the migrating era in my life in spite of hardships. (I had not talked about migrating in a very long time.) In response to my statement, the acquaintance said something that I really pondered but thought it best not to voice a response. It wasn't worth the spent energy.

I was told that the reason I thought I had enjoyed the era was because I had nothing to compare it with. In a round about way he had already said he preferred talking with educated people and I guess I wasn't one of those. He didn't even know me. I had already let that go. I could have told him he had led a dull life because as compared to mine his was dull. There he was "home", an Anglo with a high school diploma and there I was a non-Anglo ex-migrant, with a Master's Degree in Education. Not overly impressive but impressive nonetheless. But did I have something to compare migrating with? Of course I did! The belief that once a migrant always at migrant status is a misnomer, big time, in my case.

Because of the size of the family and the difficult times imposed by the depression we resorted to the next best occupation available to us, migrating, but it didn't last forever. We phased out and picked up the pieces. Some did well, others struggled and some surpassed non-migrants. I, myself, together with my family, did well. Three of my four kids hold a master degree; one holds a bachelor's and is working on a master degree. Two of them defended us during Desert Storm. That's very commendable. They and others like them sacrifice so that we may be free. Think about it. They voluntarily sign a document not knowing whether they will come home again or not. And if so will they at least come back in one piece to say the least. Mine came back thanks to God.

I read a disturbing, true statement written by a wise person who said: Joining military forces is the equivalent to writing a blank check "up to and including death." That is, definitely love, love for our Country and for Americans. And those were my babies' signatures on their respective blank "checks."

One of those who surpassed non-migrants was my sister Lupe and her family. They ended up with a very impressive dairy farm, ten out of ten high school graduates, two medical doctors, one registered nurse and different degrees in between. The acquaintance with the comment was a white, sixtyish high school graduate. How do you like that?

There should be no need to react to the acquaintance's comment about inexperience, to put it mildly, but I'll give you a synopsis anyway: During my teaching tenure I traveled enough to seminars and conventions and have seen my share of national and amusement parks. And of course I've had my share of both hot dogs and exotic meals which sometimes have an exotic fee but not necessarily an exotic taste. I have visited and lost a few dollars at casinos in the lower half of the United States and a few others. I have visited far off relatives just for pleasure. Those are worth the drive and/or air travel. Don't get me wrong my relatives are not far off they just live geographically far. And to accomplish all that I have had my share of woes, angst, anguish for non-migrant traveling like normal people. I have traveled within Mexico and have seen most of the border towns. I traveled abroad with one of my girls who knew the area and did not mince time or energy as a guide. How fortunate and educational is that?

On top of that think about higher learning experiences. I could not have been successful at acquiring my degrees without the responsibility, accountability, budget practices, commuting, loans etc that go with it. Now there I went hungry. But let me tell you. Migrating experiences which intermittently served as vacations topped some of the non-migrating vacations and higher learning experience travel. Some of the former were more pleasant, relaxing and less hurried than the latter.

Let me give you just one simple example that comes to mind. We were in Greely, Colorado harvesting some vegetable where we enjoyed the beautiful scenery, visited the sights and got to see Forth of July fireworks. We didn't have to travel far or rush "home". We were there. It was educational, enjoyable and more relaxing than some of the non-migrating vacations I have been on. So do I have something to compare migrating with? Yes. Did I miss a whole lot because of migrating? No. Do I still believe I enjoyed the migrating era? Yes, most of it.

Part 11

Marriage

Because I have talked about my children I need to mention something about my marriage and this is as good a place as any. I will not go into a lengthy or detailed story but something needs to be included because I do have four beautiful children and eight grandchildren.

The way I see it is that life on this earth isn't perfect. Maybe for some it is but I think most of us ordinarily go through some setbacks or hardships. In my case I feel lucky in that I came out ahead. I didn't have a perfect marriage but I did have four beautiful kids who are top scale and that, for me, is a very fair outcome.

Not as I pictured it though. First off I thought I would be a stay-home wife and mom. Secondly, I would have beautiful kids which I did. I would dress them nicely and feed them well as they attended school, parties and such. The cycle would then continue....get married, have kids, become grandparents. It didn't happen the way I expected as far as staying home went but I have much to be thankful for. Because even though my kids are not perfect they are as perfect as kids can be and all are someone to be very proud of. Two of them defended us during Desert Storm. Did I already tell you that? Did I tell you they're all educated?

As far as my marriage is concerned I will always look back on it with sadness but I take my share of responsibility for eventual failure. I didn't have a formal wedding and didn't get to wear a very well deserved lily white wedding gown. I did have a church ritual with two witnesses....no party, no guests, no gifts no frills. I married at twenty-two years of age, lived with my husband for twenty-eight years but didn't budget for a divorce until ten years later. He didn't have a single romantic bone in his body, and he loved to socialize with frequently.

Some of those years I spent in the marriage I felt lonely except for my four children who filled my time productively. Once the kids were out of the nest he decided he wanted the residence so we separated, he got his wish. That was one big mistake on my part but I had no choice; he had a short fuse which kept getting shorter as the years went by.

Inadvertently, my parents' rearing and familial setting partially contributed to marriage failure in my case but I didn't see that coming. What happened is that I learned responsibility and discipline from them but I didn't see that the more responsibility I undertook the more he relaxed. The more he relaxed the more he socialized. At that time friends were very important to him therefore socializing was foremost agenda. (Years later when he remarried he didn't see it as significant for his second marriage so where exactly was I amiss?) Then I imagine he saw what was happening and decided I probably didn't need him but that was a mistake on his part. Nonetheless, he felt the need to push me away rather than for me to leave him which I wouldn't have. If he had taken time to get to know me he would have known that. I would not have left him; I had promised before God that I wouldn't.

So I became the first divorced person in a long line of matrimonies. All this happened because I was totally naïve and totally unprepared to make choices I didn't even know existed. I'm not placing blame here. I'm just taking my share of responsibility for my naiveté.

I spent most of the time in the fields and disciplined by my father for twenty-two years therefore responsibility and discipline became second nature for me. So it stands to reason that after I married, not by choice but by necessity and with blinders, I emulated my father's role in the marriage but at the same time remained true to my mother's role. I fulfilled two roles and that was lame. Very early, subtly and oblivious to the fact I became head of household. I didn't realize that at the time but it worked against me anyway. I was blind, yes, but I was partially responsible for monetary contribution for my children's welfare and well being.

Unfortunately, I didn't know how to involve my husband in his share of responsibility. At home I had learned that the husband was the decision maker so I went along with whatever he decided. Even when he decided he needed to socialize rather than spend time with the family I went along with it. I also took it for granted that he knew he was head of the family but he didn't abide by it. I told you I was naïve. Please don't agree so readily or change naïve to something else. Been there done that.

The families that surrounded me while with my parents didn't help the situation either. They were not "typical" families as I learned later but that's all I knew. That left me totally vulnerable because I was not aware that different types of customs existed even in what seemed like the same culture. Within my family there was no unfaithfulness, no alcohol drinking, except for one brother, no smoking and no divorce. That sounds like a fairy tale but it's the truth.

Males on the parental side were very handsome and classy but the maternal side wasn't too far behind either which means they were tempted to stray but didn't. One very handsome uncle who didn't migrate and looked like Miguel drove an eighteen wheeler (semi) cross-country. He had the opportunity to stray and may have but I didn't learn about it so I didn't experience anything different than what I was accustomed.(I was about six when I first saw that truck in front of our house and I was very proud of it so I went out to kick the tires. I had to make sure the tires were safe for the trip and all trips after that.)

One of my paternal uncles became widowed at a very early age but didn't remarry or live with another woman. So even when it was fair and legal I didn't see or hear about another woman otherwise I would have been better prepared for a different type of setting. Their only daughter Ana was only thirteen years of age when her mom passed away. I'm sure he had many opportunities to remarry but didn't.

Oh well, what's done is done and I have to forgive myself once again for my naïve tendency. But over and above I need to commend myself for one thing, or several maybe. Because through the haze of work and household responsibilities I read, studied and contemplated continuing education.

During marriage I didn't get away from the fact that I needed the means for better employment and finally retirement other than working at the slacks factory or the front desk of a lumber yard, for instance. Persistence paid off as I eventually continued where I left off with education while working full time as an educational, bilingual paralegal. I struggled against the odds and ended up with pocket change, hungry and in debt with a student loan when I decided to attend full time for my last academic classes but that was fine because I made it through. I triumphed against all odds.

I kept up with household responsibilities so effectively that my husband didn't even realize how serious I was about acquiring a degree. I mostly attended summer sessions until the last ten months of academic college classes. When I was to receive my certificate he didn't even acknowledge or complement me on my long awaited accomplishment. I don't think even my children realized where I stood academically until I told them I was graduating but they all attended the ceremony.

Shortly after I started my teaching tenure I worked for, received a master degree and that was with honors. I enjoyed the classroom aspect of it but experienced a spectrum of administrative levels. Some administrators were great, some were conscientious and some had no business in the education field. It was too late but some of the lessons I learned would have been beneficial in my marriage but that's neither here nor there.

After retirement I substituted for a parochial and then a public school district. While there I almost rounded off my seventieth year on a workforce including schooling except for short terms for each baby but even if it was just promoting lotions and the hostess parties that went with it, I worked. I was a few months short of the seventieth mark....too bad.

If writing a book can be counted as work, that means I've reached in excess of the seventieth mark. So I need a break. And believe me when I say that at this point I feel the need and desire to relax and do nothing....absolutely, nothing. I've earned the privilege and I need some relax time. So I will relax.

Part 12
Equally Endowed or Not?

It wasn't easy to persevere during the depression or even as it dwindled but that wasn't our main concern. Because we were steered away from our language and heritage practices, dwarfism was inevitable in our cultural generation and in the forthcoming group. In order to be accepted, somewhat, the generation had to renounce the Mother tongue, adopt the accepted one and melt into a "suitable", "proper" and "appropriate" or whatever pot we needed to melt into when in our short term schooling sessions.

First the Mother tongue had to go. The language could not be spoken in public, therefore, it was considered an inferior language which needed to be renounced, eradicated. That made it embarrassing not only to speak the language but also to be associated with anyone who spoke it. Then in trying to lose the Mother tongue so abruptly and at the same time trying to learn the accepted one both languages suffered for a good while. In some instances we ended up with virtually no language at all. Some were well versed in the heritage language but were embarrassed to admit it so denied it unyieldingly.

Allow me to give you one unyielding example: The next door neighbors were cleaning the yard. A hoe was left blade up so the grandmother told the grandson to pick it up. He told her he didn't understand Spanish, didn't pick up the hoe and walked on. As he was walking back he stepped on the hoe blade and the handle hit him right in the face. In Spanish he cried out: Hay! Me di un azadonaso! The pain yanked out the Spanish in the thirteen year old. And perfect Spanish at that.

There's no exact translation for the phrase but it's close to: Ow! The hoe ricocheted and hit my face. Close enough. So did the grandson understand and speak Spanish? Duh!

We were not speaking our heritage language yet there was not much opportunity to practice or speak the only accepted language, English, so we were learning it at a very slow pace. And let's not even go into the pronunciation aspect which demanded so much adjusting to and so much more exercise from our poor vocal cords. That would require a whole other printed narrative so let's discuss that in the very far future.... maybe.

And here's another example that does not fall under unyielding but it fell under saving face. Certain items needed to be ordered in English such as food and drinks: We did not order a chocolate shake in one uninterrupted sentence for fear of a slip up so the transaction went something like this: Let me have a shake please. And from across the counter: What kind? Answer: Chocolate. We knew the difference but that was too much flapping and clutter for our poor untrained vocals. Chocolate and shake together did not work too well for some of us.

I had a supervisor in a school who said: Give me a piece of paper, please. We were friends so once I gave her a piece of paper. She said: You know what I mean. She didn't trust herself to say: A sheet of paper. She always made fun of herself and was good natured about it.

On top of all the extra vocal exercise there was a different intonation to go with the language we were expected to speak but we were too busy learning it to even notice. So then, we were criticized for what was called an accent in our meager language acquisition. Would there ever be a light at the end of the tunnel?

Now to me, the accent label seemed more like a tonal inflection than an accent default but who was I to correct the mislabeling? Was it mislabeling? According to me all languages have their own individual and unique rhythmic cadence or intonation or is it an accent or blending of both? I'm all confused. Which language is not accented or tonal? Please educate me.

So pride whether innate or learned was very difficult to hold onto with on-going bigotry and, in turn, change but some succeeded in staying afloat, thanks to parental guidance....our role models. My mother always managed to look clean and fresh. She never wore make-up, used cream or lotion but her complexion was clean, rosy and healthy looking. She didn't show wrinkles until she was over seventy-five. I know that's neither here nor there but I thought that was impressive and I think some of it goes hand in hand with pride.

My father became sweaty while working but cleaned up really well. He shaved religiously, his hair was always clean and combed during meals and outings. I never saw him grubby on or off the fields and he carried himself really well at all times....our role models.

Miguel who was also a positive role model both before and after military service, picked cotton with us for about three years only before he joined the armed forces. He was in the

Navy during late thirties and mid forties. Before that he worked alongside my father on the farm. He and one of my mother's brothers defended us during World War II. They fought alongside Americans but after they returned they were Mexicans again. Talk about another blow to the ego!

Unfortunately, the enemy didn't know that some weren't Aericans so they shot at, wounded and killed some of brown pigment. When perished "Mexican" soldiers either came or were transported home they were a separate entity again and therefore did not merit the same privileges as "Americans" veterans enjoyed or couldn't be entombed in "American" military burial grounds if their families preferred. Also they were not welcome in certain religious chapels. In addition Hispanic veterans were denied

educational, medical, housing and other benefits promised under the bill of rights. Did they not also fight for our freedom?

Luckily one of our honored leaders lobbied for reversal of denials and with much effort succeeded in reversing them. After that, fallen soldiers were entombed in rightfully deserved burial grounds and were afforded well deserved military honors. Eventually, veteran rights were also granted. We owe our leader heartfelt thanks for his dedication. Our people deserved it and he came through.

Because of bigotry and racism, justifiable respect and pride which were present in previous generations was diminished and sometimes obliterated or moribund. I'm not saying that it's totally gone or lost. I'm just saying that I haven't seen much of the regal status of conduct and carriage that was present in my parent's generation. In some of my family some of that pride is still evident. It's also evident in those who are in the pot but not melted or are pseudo simulated;

those who are culturally bona fide and bilingually steadfast it seems like. Congratulations! You made it through. Keep it up.

Although my father did not debase "Americans" there was a definite comportment which elicited respect when interacting with farmers (ninety-nine percent Anglo) whereby I felt we were not inferior or below the white race as perceived by them. How wise!

But was I above? Equal? At the time I may not have been interested or maybe too young to denote equal so what else was there other than above or below? And now it's too late to learn the answer to my curiosity from him. I know my father was proud but was he also biased?

The question is: Where was I? I had heard we were created equally endowed by a Higher Power but I hadn't learned yet about Freud, tabula rasa, the constitution etcetera but neither had many of the impressing adults we dealt with outside our realm....mainly as students. That's interesting isn't it? Are we equally endowed? What's your opinion?

Let's change the subject for a while and think about a hypothesis which plays a part in the language area: The language we gave up was not an inferior language, was it, except maybe to some. Is it not a language that is accepted or at least recognized globally....more so than others? I'm asking. In giving up the language did we not render the Nation less rich; less fortunate?

By allowing or at least ignoring interaction, play or attempted communication among students on school playgrounds would it not have been beneficial for "Americans" to naturally acquire a second language? How would it have hurt America for the majority of us to be or become bilingual or multilingual for that matter in two popular languages or more? I'm not in a position to test the logical or empirical consequence to the hypothesis and I really don't want to research at this point so I leave it up to you to agree disagree waive ponder or just let it go. That would probably be our best bet.

All I know is that according to survey studies Chinese people speak the most languages, Mexico ranks second and I don't think I want to know where we stand as a nation in the that category. My guess is that we can't be too far behind but no matter where we are we have nothing to worry about. I'm sure any nation out there will be happy to translate for us at any time for any reason and with a smile. Mexico would be a good bet. In some instances, however, we are required to take a foreign language class in school. That should help.

While I was thinking about the above, a sitcom I heard while flipping through television channels came to mind. I would like to thank the patron for the contribution but I have no idea of its source. It was supposed to be a joke but it wasn't funny. It touches negatively on one of my pet peeves now, racism. The sitcom interaction went something like this: The well to do white family had a proficient, brown bilingual maid in hire and the lady of the house took pride in bilingualism also. One evening as the maid came to the door of the room where her boss was sitting and before she had time to announce that dinner was served her boss beat her to it. She said: Yah estah sirveeda la coumeedah? And the maid answered yes and under her breath, as she turned around, continued with "Si senora, y usted habla el idioma como un idiota."

In some cases I don't blame some for being uppity or others for retaliating but it's not healthy, in my opinion. I'm assuming there were unresolved issues between these two but I'm also assuming they need each other. I wonder if by chance they could or should have shared schools, playgrounds or more and didn't. How sad.

For us as a culture, English-only was a tremendous setback when we renounced our heritage language. That was one of the strongest bonds that held us together as a family and as a culture. In halting the primary language, communication between the elder and younger generations became moribund, basically nonexistent and familial ties were virtually severed, lost. Devastatingly, the cultural wealth, influence and pride went out the door together with the rejected language. And the more isolated the younger group became from the close knit family the harder they tried to melt into the appropriate pot .What a setback! No, it was more than a setback. Because even though young children were intelligent and therefore heard, learned and understood the home language they denied it. Some eventually lost it together with the culture, customs and pride that went with it. That was unfortunate. It didn't need to happen.

In my opinion it was beneficial to retain and practice the heritage language even if it had to happen behind closed doors or away from the "norm". That may have helped the transitional process and attainment of a second language basically effortless and much more natural and profitable. In turn, heritage pride would have survived. Unfortunately kids were impressionable, tried to conform and on top of that, they were instructed by parents to listen to educators because they were their parents away from home. So what choice did they have? Obey, what else was there?

Educators, second parents, were the ones who told them not to speak their language; some of the ones who induced them to feel inferior at an impressionable age. The ones with the degree in education, yes, but did they instill cultural pride in students? No. It was the contrary. Did educational studies fail to instruct educators in the requirement of dealing with diversity in distinct areas of teaching and the ability or desire to comply? Maybe...

Even now, if some educators could hear that they were the parents away from home they would "turn in their grave". "They would turn in their grave" is a quote I hear from Anglos, themselves, when they talk about interracial marriages and other areas. I thought that was an appropriate quote to borrow even though it's not pleasant but it could hold some truth.

I cannot rightfully say that we would turn in our graves although some might I'm sure. But many of us just take into consideration that we are merely forerunners and should allow the following generation to take its course. That should work.

Part 13

Closing

According to history the Great Depression was inevitable therefore it was inevitable that our lives be disrupted for survival purposes. We left farm life and became migrant workers in my father's best interest to keep us fed and clothed. In spite of or because of that we as a family never went to bed hungry or resorted to bread lines or soup kitchens as others did during that time. We led a very simple and productive but at the same time a conglomerate life during migrating years. It proved beneficial in that we as kids spent most of the time with the family and that meant we were basically home schooled, therefore not totally exposed to the melting pot syndrome. So thanks to my parents' influence and the need to be home schooled we retained most of our cultural heritage, customs, pride and identity.

We also retained and practiced our language and transitioned effortlessly into second language acquisition by utilizing acquired basic skills and concepts. That was easy. Well not totally. Something was missing. After elementary, at least, more time spent in a school setting may have been an educational plus. Once we were secure in our own individual qualities and personalities we could have benefitted from public school education and extracurricular activities. In a sense I experienced some of the benefits and drawbacks when I attended a full academic year in the sixth grade.

I do regret not being fortunate enough to graduate from high school and not having a group to celebrate and meet with for reunions. Government intervention for students who were not able to attend full academic terms would have been helpful, beneficial and appreciated. The mandate to enroll thirteen year-olds and under no matter where we were deserved more than a band aid application. I imagine some would say that all educational responsibility fell on my parent's shoulders and maybe that's correct. I'll accept that. What's done is done.

In closing, all I would like to say to those who shared the difficult times umbrella is: Some of us were affected by a low level of national economy as a result of the depression and basically frugality was our middle name. Many of us were unduly criticized, melted or pseudo simulated in the pot and that's alright. We did what was needed or had to be done and although the depression tapered off and ended, racism is not totally at the forefront but still exists. The trick to surviving as in the past, however, is to accept our share of experiences as they occur, view them wisely, edit consciously, reject the negative and move on.

Naturally for one reason or another we may be concerned about tomorrow and that's alright, but I will let you in on a secret which I practice. I will compare it to a lay-away plan offered by some retail stores. Have you heard the term lay-away-plan? Basically, an item is selected and partial payment is required. The item remains at the store until paid in full and then possession of the item is taken.

This is how I see it: Whenever we worry we are living a form of lay-away-plan. This means we may never pay in full because there is no item to pick up except maybe stress that may lead to some type of illness, discomfort or disease if worry escalates, so relax. Practice patience. Isn't that an interesting concept to practice? Try it and you may be glad you did.

So with your permission, my advice to you is: Don't worry about tomorrow and be conscious of today or as the Spanish song dictates: "Un dia a la vez Dios mio es lo que pido de ti"; One day at a time, dear Jesus and if I may add, take one minute at a time and that should work also.

Moreover, and "by all means pat yourself on the back for all accomplishments big and small". The noted quote I borrowed from my daughter Leticia's book titled <u>Clear the Path –A Simple Approach To Eliminating Emotional Issues</u>. And she also states part of the following sentence: "Breathe deeply exhale slowly and relax" whenever you feel the need to worry. We survived the Great Depression coupled with bigotry we're here and did well so be proud. Relax.

And that's all I have for now dear readers. Thank you very much for reading my chronicle. Thank you. I hope you enjoyed reading as much as I enjoyed writing. Good bye for now.

Celia Castillo

AGAINST THE ODDS underscores a powerhouse of obstacles, difficulties and struggles of an uprooted family life from a quiet simple farm life to a humble nomad-like existence as a result of the Great Depression. In addition to a low economy, prejudice, racism and bigotry made it much more difficult to survive and succeed in an adaptive way of life; a life which became a two-fold process. One side consisted of constant moving from field to field searching for work. The second phase consisted of trying to keep up with school work and formal education in limited or short sessions. Both phases offered learning opportunities in that migrating offered vital educational experiences while formal education reinforced a different type of discipline. The different types of experiences complemented each other and allowed paramount importance if handled effectively for eventual success.